My Story Starts Here

My Story Starts Here

Voices of Young Offenders

Deborah Ellis

Groundwood Books
House of Anansi Press
Toronto / Berkeley

Groundwood Books / House of Anansi Press
groundwoodbooks.com

We gratefully acknowledge for their financial support of our publishing program
the Canada Council for the Arts, the Ontario Arts Council and the Government
of Canada.

Canada Council   Conseil des Arts
for the Arts   du Canada

ONTARIO ARTS COUNCIL
CONSEIL DES ARTS DE L'ONTARIO
an Ontario government agency
un organisme du gouvernement de l'Ontario

With the participation of the Government of Canada | Canadä
Avec la participation du gouvernement du Canada

Library and Archives Canada Cataloguing in Publication

Title: My story starts here : voices of young offenders / Deborah Ellis.
Names: Ellis, Deborah, author.
Identifiers: Canadiana (print) 20190045663 | Canadiana (ebook) 20190045701
| ISBN 9781773061214 (softcover) | ISBN 9781773061344 (EPUB) | ISBN
9781773061351 (Kindle)
Subjects: LCSH: Juvenile delinquents—Anecdotes. | LCSH: Juvenile delin-
quents—Social conditions. | LCSH: Juvenile corrections.
Classification: LCC HV9069 .E45 2019 | DDC 364.36—dc23

Illustrations by Eric Chow
Photographs by Deborah Ellis
Cover photo and text design by Michael Solomon

Groundwood Books is committed to protecting our natural environment. As part
of our efforts, this book is made of material from well-managed FSC®-certified
forests, recycled materials and other controlled sources.

Printed and bound in Canada

FSC
www.fsc.org

MIX
Paper from
responsible sources
FSC® C016245

All royalties from the sale of this book will go to two organizations that work with at-risk youth.

"There but for the grace of God go I."
— John Bradford (1510–1555), as he watched prisoners being led to their execution

Introduction

**Why can't they be like we were,
Perfect in every way?
What's the matter with kids today?**

— Lee Adams, "Kids," from *Bye Bye Birdie*

Children should obey us, trust us and amuse us. They should be grateful to us. They should allow us to feel dignified, wise, competent and powerful.

They should not defy us.

And they'd better not laugh at us.

This is a grim view of how we grown-ups see the creatures we used to be. I believe this grimness has, at least in part, formed our public policies on young offenders.

It's not all grim, of course. We adults also want to care for our young, keep them safe and pass on our hard-earned knowledge. We want the next generation to be more successful than we are. We want to save them from the mistakes we made. We want to give them every advantage, every opportunity, every chance to make good.

Some of them.

We also condemn many of the world's children to bed without supper, even to bed without a bed. We continue to buy products made by tiny underpaid hands, and we would rather pay to punish children than protect them.

Could it be that when we grow up we forget we were ever young? Do we forget how powerless we felt to create productive change in our lives? Do we not remember being confused about who we were and what we wanted? Were we never quick to make a dumb move without a thought for the consequences?

This is a book of interviews with young people who have interacted with the criminal justice system. All the names have been changed and any locations or other identifiers have been removed. I interviewed most of the young people in person. In the case of those under eighteen, I first obtained permission from their parent or guardian. A few of the interviews were done over the phone.

Many, many other individuals and agencies (including the two organizations that will receive the royalties from this book) provided me with information, advice and the means to reach out to the young people and their families, but cannot be named in the interests of protecting the identities and locations of the interviewees. The law is strict about safeguarding the identities of young offenders.

There is a First Nations community out west that has a Walk with an Elder program. Kids who are feeling lost can go up to an Elder and walk with them—not necessarily even talking—but knowing that the Elder is on their side, taking time to acknowledge them and letting the kid know they are not alone.

Many of the young people in this book talk about one person, or even one moment with one person, when a small act of kindness changed the trajectory of their lives. How often are we providing the world with kind moments—moments that could land like sunbeams on someone who desperately needs them?

Time will go by. Those who are now young will become adults who make policy. What we need now is what we have always needed—support for struggling parents, addiction-recovery help, short- and long-term steps out of poverty and access to appropriate types of education for kids who are having a hard time.

It can cost more than $100,000 a year to keep a teenager behind bars (American Correctional Association / Council of Economic Advisers, 2015). Once a child goes into prison, they are much more likely to become an adult who goes to prison.

We could turn this around with the right amount of

will in the right direction. All the resources we spend to further break broken kids could be used to help us all rise together. Think of the pain we could avoid! Think of the gifts that people could contribute if their brains are properly fed, their bodies properly housed and without recurring trauma to drag them down.

We humans made the problem of youth crime. We humans can fix it.

Kevin, 19

"When I get to a church in time for a free meal, I always ask if I can volunteer for clean-up, just so they know I can contribute. It also helps me feel this is all temporary."

Twenty percent of Canada's homeless are young people. In "Without a Home: The National Youth Homelessness Survey" (www.homelesshub.ca), most youth reported that they left home because of conflicts with their parents. Over sixty percent reported physical, emotional or sexual abuse in the home. Others reported parents who are addicted or struggling with untreated mental-health problems.

Homeless youth are four times more likely to die from things like suicide or drug overdoses. Nearly one-fifth land in some form of human trafficking (www.modernslaveryresearch.org). Without a home, all things become more difficult. How do you keep clean? Where do you do your homework? How do you eat, sleep, get out of the rain, pass the hours? Where do you keep your things?

Every year, forty thousand of Canada's young people are homeless at least some of the time. In the United States, the figure is more than two million (www.covenanthouse.org). Each one of them has a story.

I was born in a small town in New York State. I'm Native American. I was only supposed to come to Canada for a three-day visit, to meet my biological father, who I first heard about when I was thirteen. There was another guy I thought was my dad—my mother's husband—but one day him and my mom had a big argument in front of me and he said, "I'm not looking after that kid of yours anymore since he's not even mine." Then Mom fessed up about who my real dad is.

So I was up here in Canada for a three-day visit and Bio-Dad saw that I was not well. He got me a doctor and found out that I have type 1 diabetes.

Type 1 diabetes is a serious thing. Your body can't produce insulin properly, or regulate sugar properly, and you have to take good care of yourself or you could go blind, you could lose your feet. You could even lose your life. My bio-dad's family got me on the right medication and I started to feel a lot better.

It's been back and forth between Canada and the United States ever since. Bio-Dad's not really stable and Mom's life is not really what I want to be a part of. So it's been back and forth but for the last few years I've been mostly in Canada.

I'm homeless now. I've been homeless for two years.

I was living at Bio-Dad's and he said, "Go to school or go to work." I didn't want to go to school. I've got ADHD, so regular school is a struggle. With so many kids in a classroom, especially if they're racist, it's hard for me to focus. Less kids is easier for me.

I didn't really go to school in all the time I went back and forth between countries. Just here and there, now and then. I've got maybe grade ten, some grade eleven.

I went out to work doing whatever and when I got my first paycheck Dad wanted half of it to pay for my room and board. Fine, but when I got my next one he wanted more than half. When I got my third, he just pretty much took all of it. I said, "I don't need this," and I left. Bio-Dad just sits on his ass all day, soaking every cent he can out of his sugar mama. I'm not impressed by him.

The only person I can say good things about is my mother. She's a very kind, beautiful, respectable person who raised four kids without any help from a real man-father. She's in the United States still. Our

relationship is amazing but I don't want to go back to there. It's a low place for me. Makes me feel bad about myself.

Believe it or not, I have a clean criminal record. With all I've been through and done, I've never been arrested. I'd rather spend my time being free than being behind bars, so I take care not to step over the law. That's hard, to be homeless and avoid the police.

The hardest part about being homeless and having diabetes is finding food. I have my prescriptions and insulin and glucometer to test my blood sugar, but getting food is hard. The extra money I get on social assistance for a special diet is not very much when you have no fridge. You have to buy as you eat. Food-bank food is mostly for people who have kitchens. Like, they give you boxes of pasta but you can't eat raw pasta.

I live in a small city and I can sometimes get two or even three free meals a day if I can get in the right churches at the right time. Sometimes I get to a church and they've run out of food or they've changed the date of their meal or they're taking a break from serving meals. I can't always walk and walk and walk without eating because I could just drop dead right on the street. Diabetes can do that.

When I get to a church in time for a free meal, I always ask if I can volunteer for clean-up, just so they know I can contribute. It also helps me feel this is all temporary.

A permanent home would help so much. Now I carry all I own in a duffel bag. I have to haul that thing with me everywhere. I can't leave it any place because it will get stolen and then I'll have nothing, not even an extra pair of socks.

I find jobs when I can, but I have to be careful because what if I lose government help with my insulin and things? I volunteer at a youth center. I have a connection with the kids there, and seeing someone smile always makes me smile.

My life is all day by day now. Someday I'd like to travel and see the world. I'd like to be an entertainer. I do a robotic hip-hop type of dance and I do beat-box and sometimes I get hired to perform at events.

If I have a busy day of doing things in the world, I get tired and want to rest. Figuring out where to lay my head is the hard part. Sometimes I stand on the sidewalk with my duffel bag and look one way then the next. I'm just done with trying to decide which direction might get me to a safe place for the night.

If I were going to give advice to kids in my situation, I'd say don't give up. If you give up and decide your life is always going to be like this, you won't make it. Believe me. I know what I'm talking about. You have to believe there is something good out there waiting for you. I've been in this struggle for two years and I will not give up.

?

- What causes chaos in families?
- What qualities make a great parent? How can you build those qualities in yourself? How can you contribute those qualities to the family you are in now?

Taking Steps ...

For yourself

Kevin has type I diabetes, which people are born with. Type 2 diabetes can be caused, in part, by a poor diet. Add one new nutritious food to your eating plan, and put down one unhealthy choice.

For others

Learn the signs of distress for someone with diabetes and how to help them.

Volunteer at your local food bank or free supper, or do a food drive to set up a food bank at your school.

Hassan, 17

"To stay friends with them and keep the bullying away, I had to get caught up in their ways."

Someone who bullies others uses threats, insults and physical violence to make themselves feel more powerful. Bullying is also done by spreading rumors, by keeping others out of groups and by endless tiny acts meant to destroy the self-confidence of the target. Sometimes kids who have been bullied when they were small start to bully others as soon as they get bigger. In schools around the world, kids have to put up with the sort of behavior from their peers that, if it were done by adults to other adults, would result in criminal charges.

Hassan's experience with bullying started him on his journey into the justice system.

I was born in Ethiopia. I came to Canada with my family when I was six. My parents decided to leave Ethiopia because of war and other troubles. We lived on the outskirts of Addis Ababa, the capital city. I remember it was a busy place. It seemed that more women worked there than the guys. Women worked everywhere, selling things on the street, doing whatever. Mom was one of those street sellers. She sold lots of little things, anything she could buy cheap and sell for a bit more. I remember her selling air freshener. She went out to work and

Dad stayed home with us kids. I have six sisters and one brother. I am the oldest of the brothers and I have two older sisters.

My parents already had some family in Canada and they got on an official plan that the family here could bring family from over there. We flew into Toronto and someone drove us to a city a few hours from Toronto. We stayed in a sort of home you go into when you are straight off the boat, some sort of home for new people coming into the country.

I think we arrived at night. I remember being surprised the next morning when I woke up and went outside and everything was so green, so beautiful. Where we had been living in Addis was brown and dusty. I was not used to seeing so much green. It was mind-blowing.

Mom doesn't work here in Canada. She stays at home. Dad works out in another province. He was able to get a job out there so that's where he went.

I didn't know any English when I got here. My language was Ethiopian. Since I've been here I've lost most of my Ethiopian. I speak mostly English now.

I remember school being very welcoming to me. The teachers were kind. They took their time to help me. The work I did at school in Ethiopia was very different from what they studied in Canada, but the teachers helped me catch up. Things were good at that school, but then we moved to a new area when I was in grade three. I changed schools and that's when it all started.

This is when I met the bad influences in my life, on this new street and in this new school. There were all these kids just a little older than me roaming around the streets on their own. They looked strong and like they could do what they wanted.

I watched these kids all the time, the way they were comfortable being outside all on their own. I watched them do drug deals. I watched the police go after them. It was fascinating to me.

I was just starting to make friends in grade three at my old school. Then we moved and I had to start again in this new school. What happened was that the kids started to bully me. They could see I was on my own so I was an easy target for them.

The bullying was hands-on. They put their hands on me, they hit me with weapons, they made fun of me.

I didn't react. I was too stunned! I didn't know what was happening. Kids didn't bully each other at my old school. This was all new to me, to have kids treat me like that.

I didn't defend myself. I didn't know how. It kept getting worse. They saw me as someone to attack. It got so much worse as we got older and the other kids got bigger.

The teachers knew. I told them but they didn't believe me, or they pretended not to. The bully kids had a lot of friends and the teachers didn't want to make trouble for themselves.

By grade six I was at that point where I was having enough of it. I was tired of being scared every day when I went to school. Every day!

One day in middle school the main kid who had been bullying me all these years came at me again and this time I fought back. I got beat, but after that I had the guy's respect. He decided we could be friends and the bullying stopped. He got his gang to agree.

To stay friends with them and keep the bullying away, I had to get caught up in their ways. So I was sort of forced into it, but I also liked having friends and adventures and not being beat up every day!

In grade eight I started smoking cigarettes because everyone else in the group was doing that. During the summer after grade eight I went from cigarettes to booze and pot. One of the older guys in the group would provide us with all the stuff. I don't know where he got it. I had my ideas.

Nobody in my family knew this was going on with me. It's like that in most families, I think. Nobody talks. The parents lie to their kids and the kids lie to their parents and everyone is on their own.

My parents are straight up, always were. They're like,

pay your way, don't take what's not yours, work hard, do your part.

I was doing all this drinking and smoking and escaping from the house in the middle of the night to run the streets, looking for excitement. I got caught up in listening to music that some people consider damaging to kids, with lyrics full of hate and drugs and violence. I took that message as my own, you know, that all police hate all black people and you have to take what you want because no one will let you have anything good if you don't just grab it.

The first time I got officially in trouble happened that summer.

We were chilling in the back of a field, like a vacant lot, where there were no adults. Some rent-a-cops came. I guess it was their field. They searched a guy and found marijuana. The rent-a-cops took the grass and we all ran in different directions. It showed me what could happen, and that the people I was hanging with would not help me if there was trouble.

During that summer I went back to Ethiopia with my family, the first time we'd been back since we moved to Canada. I was thinking about going back for the longest time. It was a relief to be back there but also a disappointment. Things had changed. The people I missed were not there anymore, but the air was still the same. The good feeling of home was still there. We spent three months in Ethiopia. I was two months late starting back to school.

Another new school, high school this time. I'd had a long break from those bad-influence friends but the bad stuff was still in me.

Someone's cellphone was sitting on a table at school. I didn't see anyone around, so I took it. The hall camera saw me. The next day the vice-principal called me into the office. The police were there. They asked me about the phone. I played it cool, then they showed me the tape. I gave the phone back and got a warning.

There's a mall near this school. One day I went there with some friends, to the Superstore. I had this bag with me with an open zipper on it. My friend dropped video games into my bag. I didn't catch on until he had put, like, three games in my bag.

I said to him, "You must be on dog food," and I gave him the bag. I wasn't going to be the one walking out of the store with stolen stuff.

My twelve-year-old cousin was with us. He was acting stupid. He grabbed a game, put it down his pants and started running out of the store. I took off running after him because I was sort of responsible for him. My whole crew ran out of the store and kept running.

I hopped on my bike and zoomed away but the police caught my cousin. I knew they'd make my cousin tell, so I went back to the store where the police were holding him. We gave back the games and apologized and the police gave me my second warning.

The summer between grade nine and ten me and my friends went to Shoppers. This was right at the end of summer and the Hallowe'en stuff was up. I was looking at costumes. I saw a mechanical witch stirring a pot. I goofed around. I put a cowboy hat on my head and danced with this witch, just to have fun.

My friends up and ran out of the store and I ran out

Taking Steps ...

For yourself

Have you ever been bullied? Do you still hold on to some of the negative messages bullying gave you? What can you do to replace them with positive messages about yourself?

Did you ever bully someone else? Examine why, and, if you can, apologize to that person.

For others

Do you know of a kid at your school who is being bullied? Think of one thing you can do to make their day easier, then do it. Bullying is a behavior that needs many people working together to stop it.

with them, totally forgetting I had the stupid hat on my head. Once I realized, I turned around and took a step back to the store to take the hat back, but the security guard was already right there. He grabbed me and called the police.

The police gave me my third warning. Then they drove me home and told my parents. My parents sure yelled at me!

I settled down after that and didn't really do anything wrong for the next couple of years. I went to school, got good grades. Just, you know, lived. Then, a week ago I did something stupid again.

It was on Senior Skip Day. I was planning to go to the beach with a bunch of other kids but my plans didn't work out.

I was at school, feeling lousy because I was almost the only one there. Everyone else was having a great beach day. I thought, "I'm just gonna go home." I didn't want to walk. I found an unlocked bike at the back of the school. I rode the bike part of the way home to a convenience store. I bought a drink and left the bike there.

Two days later, the police, a translator, the vice-principal, Mom, Dad and my uncle were all in the office waiting for me. The police said they had me on a security camera taking the bike.

In the back of my mind I'm like, "Not again, not again, not again."

I told everyone I lost the bike and didn't know where it was.

The police said, "You've been given too many warnings," and they gave me a date to go get a mugshot. I was charged with theft under $5000. The officer was the one who had given me warnings before. He said, "I know you're basically a good guy but this is now out of my hands. If you can find and return the bike, we'll put it on the form for the judge."

So now I have a date to go to court—the same date as my eighteenth birthday!

- Have you ever felt forced to go along with others, even though something inside you was telling you not to?
- Is there something you would like to ask your parents to help you understand them better? Is there something you wish they would ask you?

I've got to really think now about what I do. No more games. Just the other day I walked by somewhere and saw a shoulder bag someone had left on a bench. I went through it and found a phone, a really nice one. I said to myself, "I could take this phone and make a quick few dollars out of it." I didn't think about that too long. I dropped the phone back into the bag and walked away.

I know how to make a good choice. I just have to do it.

I think the biggest thing that helps me right now is being Muslim. I've gotten more into my religion in the past couple of years. Islam teaches us to respect ourselves, not to act in a way that would disrespect others or bring disrespect down on ourselves. I've learned how to discipline myself with the Ramadan fast and staying away from alcohol. When I go to the mosque I find peace in my deep soul. I know that one day I will have to stand before God and answer questions about my behavior. That will keep me on the straight path.

I like being useful. I like helping with the community potluck suppers and doing school clean-up. It gives me joy to be busy and useful and I won't be either of those things if I go to jail.

I think that kids commit crimes when they don't feel like they fit in anywhere. Maybe you should call this book "The Misfits."

A Mother's Story

We were a typical family with things that went awry.

My son who got in trouble is the youngest of four. They are all close in age. We raised them all the same. My husband and I are both professionals. We were always on the same side of parenting decisions. We were hands-on parents. We had rules but not awful ones. For example, we always had family dinners and put more emphasis on family activities than on technology.

Before our son went to middle school, everything

was good. He was very involved with sports. His grades were good.

He and two of his friends applied to go into a gifted program for middle school, the same program his older brother got into. His two friends got in. He didn't. That really bothered him. He had assumed he'd get in—truly, he's very smart—and when he didn't, I think he didn't know how to think about it.

We sent him to French immersion for grade seven and eight, and that was the first time I saw him cry after school. He didn't know anyone, didn't know French, and he just felt out of place. But time went on and he seemed to settle in.

He's always been a forgetful child. He'd come home with someone else's shoes on. He forgot to bring a note home for his eighth-grade school trip so he didn't get to go. We kept thinking he would learn from these incidents but he never seemed to.

In ninth grade he got in with a certain group of kids. My husband and I took our first trip away in nineteen years. My husband's parents stayed with our kids. We got a call from them that our son was caught stealing. He got caught a second time and then he got suspended. A month later we got a call from a neighbor who owns a store. Our son was seen on a security camera, stealing a box of chocolate bars. At the end of grade nine he got caught smoking weed.

My husband and I were involved with all this from the beginning. We were not parents who looked the other way. When he didn't come home when he was supposed to, we'd jump in the car and go looking for him. We were *involved*.

It became a weird spiral over grade ten. He wasn't going to classes. Then we found out that he'd blocked calls coming into our house from the school. He brought his friends over to smoke weed in our basement before we went to church on Christmas Eve. He became less consistent with his sports teams and was kicked off one that he had been given an award for the year prior.

I did not ignore things. We searched his bags often and

found weed, bongs and once a scale, so we knew he was probably selling drugs as well as using them.

We tried to get him into a new environment, thinking that might help. We talked to him about private school. He let us put in the application and went to visit the place for a day—and he seemed to kind of like it. We later found out that the night before he went to the private-school interview he left the house during the night and he and two friends stole another kid's backpack and credit card and tried to use the card. He was caught.

He got a pre-charge for that and put into a diversion program. He had to pay $300 from his own money to pay back for the stolen laptop in the backpack and he had to help out with the basketball program at the YMCA.

My husband and I refused to pay for a lawyer for him. We said, "If you want to do this behavior, then you deal with the consequences."

We helped in other ways. We did show up in court to give him emotional support and we drove him to the Y, for example. We met with psychologists, got him drug tested and tested for learning problems. But unless someone wants to change …

He completed diversion, and then things got really bad in grade eleven. He went to school mostly only for phys ed. He started smoking weed in the house, coming home at three in the morning on school nights, or going to bed then leaving during the night. One of his friends—whose parents are university professors, smart people—had a room up a fire escape in their house where all the kids would go any time of the day to smoke dope. We begged the parents to shut it down and they wouldn't.

It was a horrible Christmas that year. So much chaos. I couldn't sleep for worrying about him.

He was arrested for spray painting his nickname on the courthouse with his friends. He was caught with the paint! He was in the police car in front of our house in the middle of the night. I started talking with his friends. He yelled at me to stop. I yelled back at him. I'm outside in my pajamas, yelling at my son who's in the back of a police car. It was all madness.

My husband and I went to different therapists to try to deal with all this better. We were prepared to send our son anywhere we could to get him help—one place we looked at would have cost us $100,000—but he refused to go.

It came down to us saying, "If you're going to stay at home, you need to get help." He refused, so we said he had to leave.

It was pouring that day. He packed a duffel bag. I made sure he knew where the food banks and shelters were, and off he went. We cried. It was awful. We later found out that he stayed with various friends.

Meanwhile, he was accepted into another diversion program. He managed to get himself there and he was matched up with a mentor he really liked. He agreed to go to summer school—a chemistry course! We got him a bus pass, he got himself to school and he passed with a seventy!

He went to the principal of the high school that had kicked him out and asked to be let back in. The principal agreed, with conditions, and he graduated.

It wasn't all easy. Every day there was something, some crisis, more suspensions, and a lot of tolerance from the vice-principal. But he graduated. He tried college for a few months this year but wasn't able to manage. That was when he realized he was using weed to cope with life but it was actually making things worse. He quit college, moved home, worked hard to get off weed, found a job at a hardware store where for the first time someone understood him (the owner of the store). I am extremely proud of him.

His behavior has been very hard on the family. For a long time his brothers could not relate to him. His sister felt she got short-changed on our attention because so much of our focus was on him.

Our son had been very outwardly confident and independent until he was not accepted into the gifted program. He had not had to deal with any adversity up to that point, and we wondered whether, when it came, that he did not know how to handle it. His self-esteem suffered and he went searching for a new way to fit in.

Ian, 17

"When you start to think about the people you're hurting, it makes it harder to do it."

High-school dropouts are more likely to end up in prison than those who graduate. The lack of education is the second-biggest way (next to previous incarceration) to predict whether someone will end up in jail (Canadian Council on Learning, 2009).

Kids who end up in the foster care system can have a difficult time sticking it out to the end of high school. They might get moved to many different foster homes, go in and out of the chaos of their own home, and each time they move, they have to change schools. Maybe they'll miss the lessons on long division or maybe they'll never be in one school long enough to get the help they need with reading.

I've been in five different foster homes. The one I'm in now I've been in for three years and four months. The foster mom I've got now is wonderful. She brought me here today to talk with you and she shows me all the time that she cares about me and about what I do and what happens to me.

I've completed grade ten, heading into grade eleven next month. I don't have any favorite subjects. I do all right in all of them.

My trouble with the law started in grade four. Me and some friends started fires in our town.

There were some caves in the area where I was living. We liked to explore the caves and we thought it would be great to have campfires there. We gathered up some branches off dead trees and made a fire and it was fine.

We might have been okay if we'd left it there. I mean, we should have known more about fire safety, but I don't think we were bothering anybody. But we decided to keep building fires and to build bigger ones.

It's against the law to start fires like that. People caught on that it was us because we needed paper to build these fires. We would go to those free-newspaper and free-magazine stands and empty these out and run down the street with armloads of these things. It was a small town. People knew us, got to wondering what we were doing, put two and two together and called the police.

We got arrested but because we were so young we just got a lecture and a slap on the wrist and then got taken home. I got in trouble at home. Grounded, couldn't have matches, that sort of thing.

I got into more serious trouble in grade nine. I didn't like school and skipped it all the time. This one day we skipped classes the whole day, then came back into the school to catch the bus home.

We were walking through the halls goofing around, and we walked right into the principal. We were high. The principal searched us, found our joints and rolling papers. He called the cops. They came and took our stuff, including a little knife we had on us. They took that too but they didn't formally charge us. But they took our names and gave us a "next time" warning.

That principal never liked me. The police didn't charge us but the principal suspended us—two months!—for just that little bit of drugs. After the suspension was over, he said he didn't want us back in his school.

My parents split up when I was young. It was not a good breakup. Lots of yelling and fighting. It was bad. I went with Mom but she had a breakdown so I couldn't stay with her. Dad couldn't take me. He was breaking under the strain of everything. He didn't know how to care for me, or maybe he knew how but knew that he couldn't, or maybe he just didn't want to.

I was put in foster care.

It was brutal. I was a little kid and my parents were falling apart and I was plopped down into this strange house with strange people who said, "Here! Live! Be good!" There were two other kids already living there so I had to get along with them too.

You think that's easy? You try it.

I stayed there for a bit. Then they moved me to a different foster home. Then they moved me again. Each move

The Power of a High-School Diploma

In the United States, one out of every ten male high-school dropouts ends up in prison, jail or youth detention. For African Americans, the rate is one in four. For men who graduate high school, the incarceration rate is one in thirty-five ("Study Finds High Rate of Imprisonment Among Dropouts," *New York Times*, 9 October 2009).

It is impossible to separate racism from these facts, and Black and Indigenous young people are especially vulnerable to being passed through the system without proper numeracy or literacy skills. Only 35 percent of First Nations, Métis and Inuit students graduate high school — less than half the general population (Chiefs Assembly on Education, Assembly of First Nations, 2012). Many communities are too small to have their own high school, and distances are so huge that students have to leave their families and travel far away, just to attend school.

Dropping out of school narrows someone's economic possibilities and lowers self-confidence. A high-school diploma does not solve all problems, but not having one makes those problems bigger.

If you are struggling in high school, get help. If the first ten adults you ask don't help you, keep asking. Someone will do the right thing. If regular high-school is not working for you, find an alternative. Form a club with others who hate school to figure out a way to get through it. Don't cheat yourself out of what is your right. Don't cheat yourself out of a better future. Don't let the jail-builders win.

(With thanks to "Preventing Jail with Diplomas" by Mimi Williams, *Vue Weekly*)

was hard, being with new people and new sets of rules.

When I was sixteen I got charged with B and E [break and enter]. I got put on probation for a year and I had to spend a week in open custody.

Open custody was not really open because I couldn't leave. They set the bedtime, and it was very early. You couldn't use knives. They had very specific rules and if you broke one of those rules they wouldn't let you play video games or go outside.

I did a lot more B and E's than the one I was charged with. They were all about getting me money for weed. Me and my friends would walk around town looking for easy places to get into, going into cars that weren't locked or shops or houses or whatever. I never thought I would get caught.

I never thought about the people I was stealing from. I just thought about getting something for myself. When you start to think about the people you're hurting, it makes it harder to do it. I think if I *had* thought about them, I wouldn't have broken into their places and taken their stuff. It must have made them scared and upset, and I don't want to be the guy that makes people feel like that.

My family now is all spread out. I have two brothers and one sister. One brother is in one province far from this one and my sister is in another province. Another brother is in this province but far away from here. I learned that my real father left me as soon as I was born and the man I thought was my real father was my adopted dad. I talked to my birth dad just two times in my life. If he's not interested in me, I'm not interested in him. I'd like to see my brothers and sister, though.

My foster mom, the one I have now, says I can stay with her even after I turn eighteen. Children's Aid might pay for my education. I don't know if I can do school anymore but maybe they'll help me learn a trade. I have a job now at a place that replaces car windshields and I like doing that. Maybe they'll keep me on.

I have this thing in my head that tells me that as soon

?

- How might the chaos in Ian's life lead him to feeling lost?
- What might raise his expectations of what he can have and achieve?

as something good happens, it's all going to get ruined. It's hard not to give up on myself. I feel like there's something deep inside me that won't let me do anything good. I wear myself out worrying that something bad will ruin something good so I can't really enjoy those better moments.

I've been having blackouts, so bad that they took my driver's license away. The doctors don't know why this is happening. I think I'm probably okay but the doctor doesn't. He's got me on a rush list for tests but they're still four months away.

The Children's Aid still has my birth certificate and my health card. They treat you like they own you. When they come into meetings with you, that's their attitude. They own you.

Who am I? I'm lost.

Taking Steps ...

For yourself

Do you ever feel lost? What can you put into your life that is positive and that you can rely on when times get difficult?

For others

Is there a subject in school that you're good at? Help out a student who is falling behind, or help tutor kids in younger grades.

Deanna, 18

"They hurt me and no one cared. If I did that to someone, I'd be charged."

Sometimes parents are abusive, actively hitting and verbally attacking their children. Some parents are neglectful, which means they do not give their children what they need — physically, medically, educationally or emotionally. Children who are emotionally neglected can grow up feeling lonely, unwanted, unloved and believing they have no value. They may make poor choices in relationships because they have no information about what a healthy relationship looks like (www.abusewatch.net).

I was eight, I think, when I went into my first foster home.

Just because my parents didn't take good care of me didn't mean I never wanted to see them again. Of course I wanted to see them. They were my parents! I told the foster mom one day that I was going to go see my dad and then I just left.

She later lied and said I never told her. She called the police and said I was missing. The police found me and forced me into a group home because they said I was a runaway risk. They couldn't trust me to stay in a foster home.

Foster homes are different from group homes. In a foster home you live with a family that's not your own. You live with different kids, often not your own brothers and sisters. Some of them belong there and some are foster kids like you. You kind of join the family and do what they do.

A group home is more structured and there are staff who come in and out. A group home has levels. If you do what they tell you, you can earn community time, like you earn the privilege of going to the mall. If you don't do your chore you get taken off privileges for twenty-four hours. No TV, no outings, no phone. They're all different. One group home I was in had a top level where you could earn money by doing extra chores.

Some group home staff are good and kind. Others, you can tell they went into this work because they were too stupid or lazy to do anything else and they treat it like babysitting. They manipulate the kids. I've heard some say things like, "You'll never succeed" and when the kid talks back they take away privileges.

I kept getting arrested. Sometimes you get arrested and they let you go with a warning. The first time I got charged was for assault when I was thirteen. I've had six assault charges. One of them was assault with a weapon which I'll tell you about in a second. I've had lots of breach-of-condition charges. Every time I'd run away they'd hit me with another breach charge.

The assault with a weapon. I was in a group home. It was dinner time. We were having chili or stew or spaghetti sauce. I was putting food on my plate and the grease spattered on the staff next to me and she pressed charges. That's my assault with a weapon. The lawyer said I was stupid for pleading guilty but I didn't want to go to jail. I thought they'd go easier on me if I pled out.

I did a course where they get you to think about what you did. If you complete the course and other conditions the charges go away. It works for some.

I remember walking into court on my first charge. I was

- What would you hate the most about being locked up?
- What life skills do you need to be able to function in the world as an independent adult? Do you have all those skills? How can you learn the ones you need to know?

thirteen, and I was shorter than I am now. I had to walk up stairs into court from the cells, up the stairs on my short legs in shackles and with my hands cuffed behind my back. I couldn't do it. The guards picked me up and dragged me into court. They hurt me and no one cared. If I did that to someone, I'd be charged.

I've been in and out of jail and group homes. The last group home I was in had custody levels. On Free Status you have the most freedom and privileges, but you still have to ask permission to do anything. On Limited Supervision you have a lot of rules and restrictions. On CS or Constant Supervision, you're watched all the time. It's a group home for kids who have done a lot of running away or a lot of crimes.

The director of this group home really saved me. We had a good connection but I didn't like being there. I ran away from there on April Fool's Day. I got away almost to this other town when I got a text message from her. It said, "I'm sorry you're not here. You'll miss my goodbye party."

I really liked her and didn't know she was leaving, so I went back to the group home to say goodbye and she said, "April Fool's!"

She knew that if I ran away again, I was going to be sent to a secure custody place, and she said, "I want you to do good and not go to jail." She took a risk for me. She was supposed to report me and she didn't.

Open-custody group homes and places—they have no lock on your bedroom so they don't lock you in a cell. You can help make dinner, even use knives when the staff is with you. You can go on supervised outings and you can stay up late one night a week to watch movies.

When you go into open custody, you're searched. You have to take your clothes off and they inspect you, but you get to keep a towel on.

Secure custody—all the doors are locked. You are in jail. When you go in, they search you, no towel, open your legs and squat.

I never thought about the people on the receiving end

of my assaults. I was too caught up in how *I* was feeling and my anger to think about the impact on others. On my eighteenth birthday I got a rude awakening. I had money stolen from me and also a pair of amusement park passes.

The thieves took every cent I had. I remember standing on a street corner with five minutes left on my phone, calling a cousin for help.

This cousin picked me up. She drove all the way from another town to get me. I broke down crying in her arms. I thought, maybe I do have some decent family after all.

I don't talk to my mom anymore. There's no point at this stage. Maybe in the future. I'm talking to my dad these days and we have a pretty good connection.

Now I'm eighteen and trying to make it on my own.

I have to say that group homes make it harder. It's not real life. You don't learn what you need to learn to get on in life. Like buying groceries. The staff would take us grocery shopping but we couldn't pick anything. The staff made the list, they made the decisions and they handled the money. We were just along to carry the bags. They rarely asked us what we wanted to eat. Okay, some people think, you kids are in a sort of prison, so why should you get to choose what you want to eat? But group homes are mostly for kids who are just kids. Not all the kids in them are criminals. I didn't think anything about it at the time, but when I had to go buy groceries for myself I was shocked at how much things cost! I had no idea how to budget or what to buy.

I have four more credits to go and then I will be finished high school. I'm going to go to college to be a child and

Taking Steps …

For yourself

Learn how to go grocery shopping, how to plan meals, make a list, find bargains and stick to a budget.

For others

Once you know how to shop, take on this task for your family.

youth worker. Then I'm going to get a job at one of my old group homes and see if I can do it better for the next bunch of lost kids than was done for me.

Kirk, 19

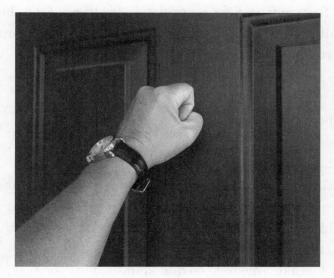

"Once you get into the system it's really easy to stay in it."

When we're children, we look for examples of how to behave. We mimic those older than ourselves, especially those we love. Boys without good men in their lives struggle to learn how to grow into good men themselves.

When I was fifteen I was part of a very successful marijuana-delivery business.

The way it would work was people who wanted drugs—mostly marijuana because that was the easiest to get—would call this number and place their order and we'd deliver it and collect their money. I was the runner. The driver would stay in the car and sometimes park or sometimes drive around so they wouldn't be sitting ducks for the cops.

I'd take the drugs, get out of the car, deliver them to the customer, collect the money, then get back in the car.

There were times I'd be out on the street with lots of money in my pocket, waiting for the driver to come back and get me and thinking, "I could just keep all this money and take off." I never did it though. I'm not stupid.

You never knew who would answer the door. Someone I

know was stung that way. The cops placed a phony order and grabbed him at the door. He had no defense for that one. Or you'd get a party full of drunk guys who'd just grab the drugs from you and not want to pay for them. Then I'd have to call people and it would get ugly. They kept me out of that part since I was just a kid.

This lasted almost a year. I was paid a hundred bucks a night.

Then one day we were out doing a delivery when the cops drove up right in front of us, across the front of our car, and then another car cut us off in back. We were trapped. They pulled the driver out of the car and he was hanging onto the steering wheel and yelling, "Let me put it in park! Let me put it in park!" because he didn't want it ramming the cop car.

The cops yanked me out too and slammed my face against the car hood while they put the cuffs on me behind my back.

I got a fine, six months' probation and I was forbidden from having a cellphone. All the money I made was gone. I blew a lot but had a lot left that the police took because it was profits of crime.

The driver was a friend of mine. He was gay and the funniest guy you'll ever meet. I was living with him at the time. He was over eighteen so he was charged as an adult.

I was kept in a holding cell for eight hours and I went kind of psycho in there. Guys were screaming, shaking the bars. It was crazy and scary. I had to go in front of a justice of the peace. It was the first time I'd been in a court room, and man, you sure know who the power is in that place!

My friend who I was living with was also in court and they weren't going to let him out. I was afraid of where they would put me and I was afraid for my friend because being in jail if you're gay is not where you want to be. So I begged and promised and we ended up getting released together on a promise to appear in court for trial.

My parents separated when I was really young and my mom got custody of me. She had a rough ride with men

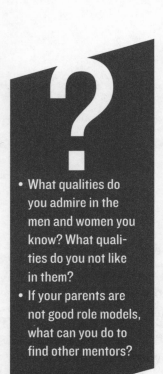

- What qualities do you admire in the men and women you know? What qualities do you not like in them?
- If your parents are not good role models, what can you do to find other mentors?

and with me. She's my role model now. If I go through tough times, I remember that she is strong and I can be too. Mom has a busy life now but I know she loves me.

Anyway, that was the start of it. Once you get into the system it's really easy to stay in it. They give you conditions to follow and if you miss even one of them you get charged with breach of conditions and that's more punishment. You start to think you'll never get out of trouble so why try?

I ended up in group homes and in and out of trouble. Food was always a problem in group homes. I was always hungry. I'd sneak food from the kitchen and get punished for it. I went back to live with my mom. That didn't work. I went to live with Dad in another city. That didn't work out either.

All these kids I've known who brag about getting arrested and how tough they were. Don't believe it. The first time I was arrested I cried like a little baby. Later I told everyone, "Oh, I was top dog in jail," to make myself look good, but it would have been better to just say, "Yeah, I was scared, I was so scared."

The drug-delivery business was so successful and went on for so long that I just felt I was going to a regular job. Some kids deliver newspapers, I delivered drugs. I just stopped thinking it was a crime, so when I got arrested I felt really sorry for myself, but really I should have seen it coming.

No, that's not completely true. I had this gut feeling

that it was going to go bad, but I kept thinking, "I'll just do one more night or one more week. I've been lucky so far, I'll be lucky again."

And I was lucky. Until I wasn't.

Now I'm aiming to go to college to get some business education and eventually open up a computer shop. I'm really good at computers. I can build them and get them running for people. I've already proven I can be part of a successful business!

I have two sons now. Having my boys has changed everything. I realize that I have to be a daddy instead of being behind bars. If I'm charged now as an adult, I'll do serious time, and I can't afford to lose my boys. I know what it's like to try to grow up as a boy without a good man around all the time to show me the right way to live. If you don't have that, it's easy to get taken in by others who don't have the best for you in mind.

Taking Steps ...

For yourself

Can you think of ways you can earn money without getting into trouble?

For others

Kirk says it would have been better to admit to other kids that he was scared in prison. Sometimes those moments of being honest can be very valuable to someone else. Watch for times when you could contribute such a moment. Being honest about who you are could help someone else be honest, too.

Voice of Experience: Victor, 26

I grew up with my mom. I never met my dad until I was eighteen. I was incarcerated when I was sixteen, and when I came home from prison, that's when I met my dad for the first time.

My mom is an immigrant from the Dominican Republic. We were homeless when I was really young. I mean, we were living on the streets. Mom's will was just strong enough to get enough money to feed us, but we didn't have money for a place to stay. We'd go into a building and sleep under the stairs there. She was always worried about getting caught.

It got so bad that she sent me to the Dominican to live for a few years. When I got back—I was born here —— Mom had gotten it together enough to find us an apartment. She had a job and everything was doing okay. Not perfect. The place was in a really bad area. I saw things on the street I wasn't supposed to see as a little kid. The rent was almost everything she earned, so my older brother and me had to find some way to work to earn money so we could eat. The way we found, because we were little kids—I was like nine or ten—was to sell drugs.

I didn't have a role model. No father figure to tell me right from wrong. I started thinking the illegal way was the right way.

The police were always around my family. We were so poor, always involved in crime, so the police were always around, watching us. The detectives used to always knock on our door, looking for my brother.

When I was sixteen they arrested me and I got tried as an adult. Man, I saw some harsh craziness in jail. People hanging themselves, getting attacked. At first I never even knew that they had a place like that where they would put adolescents. It messed me up in a bad way. I was really scared.

I got out of that but then I was dealing with adjustment back into the community. Being hurt and committing crimes was all I knew. At nineteen I got incarcerated again, for robberies and drugs. It was the same thing, people hanging themselves, hurting other people. I saw people in there with life sentences! I just did not see myself doing that, spending my life being told when to shower, when to eat, what to eat.

I started to ask myself some questions. Why was I in this situation? Was this something I was willing to keep putting myself through and keep putting my family through? Every time they came to visit me they'd see me in these disgusting clothes. Is this who I wanted to be? I started to face up to the challenges of what I needed to do to be a better me. I had been waiting for someone else to help me with my problems, but no one was coming. I was the only one who could do it.

I started reading, everything I could get my hands on. One of my favorite books is *The Secret*, which talks about what you put into the world is what you get back. I used to think so negative all the time, and that's what I got back. When you're in prison, there is so much you can't control, but you can control your attitude. I started laughing and smiling more. It made a difference.

When I got out I was accepted into this food truck program for former inmates. They teach you working skills and make you realize you can be different in the world. Now I am a community organizer for others who end up in prison, to help them and their families go on a better road. I've had newspaper articles written up about me and the campaign.

The world tends to incarcerate people and throw away the key before anyone realizes the full potential of some-one. We put a wall around them before they can really shine. There may be people wasting in prison right now who could have been scientists, for example, and find a cure for cancer or AIDS. If we put more money and energy into supporting families when kids are young, we won't have to spend so much locking kids up when they get older.

I was able to face the demons of everything I have been through. I believe I am here for a purpose, and I am finding out that purpose through reading and thinking and working out and working for others. I'm trying to help my mom see that she is important in the world.

No matter what you are going through, and you are about to do something you know is wrong, take a second and ask yourself, "Is this something I'm going to regret five years down the line, or is this something I will be proud of doing five years down the line?" It will help you make the right choice.

Dwayne, 19

"An adult beats up another adult, he gets charged. An adult punches a six-year-old in the face, he gets off, no problem."

Anger is emotional and it is also physical. When we get angry, our adrenal glands send out stress hormones and adrenaline. We get a burst of strength and energy. Our breathing gets faster, our heart rate goes up and the pupils in our eyes get bigger. It takes effort to think rationally. Frequent bouts of anger can put us at greater risk for heart attacks. Chronic anger can lead to depression, sleep problems, high blood pressure, headaches and stomach problems. The brain can get so used to anger, it can feel unnatural to not be angry.

Anger can come out of being wronged and feeling powerless to fix it. Dwayne's life has been full of pain and chaos and, as a result, anger.

I used to live in a group home and it was when I was living there that I got involved with the criminal justice system.

I was living with Dad. When I was six, my stepbrothers came by the house. We were playing something, with my cars, maybe. Probably making noise. Dad got mad at me. He sent me to my room. He said, "Don't come out!" Of course, I did. When he saw me outside my room he grabbed me and choked me and punched me in the face.

I was all marked up when I went to school the next day. A teacher called Children's Aid.

Dad was never arrested or charged. An adult beats up another adult, he gets charged. An adult punches a six-year-old in the face, he gets off, no problem.

Children's Aid contacted my mom to see if she wanted to take me and Mom said no, that she wasn't fit. That was probably the right decision. I can say that now, but boy, it sure hurt back then.

Children's Aid took me to a temporary foster home. All foster homes are temporary but some are places where kids get plopped for a few days in an emergency while Children's Aid looks around for a place that will keep them longer. These temporary foster parents took me on a little trip with them, just to another town to see some relatives, I think, but they didn't have permission from the Children's Aid to do that. I just remember that my worker showed up the next day and there was a big argument and she took me to a new foster home.

These new foster parents were wonderful, kind and really gentle. They made me feel like they wanted me to be in their home with them.

I was scared. I was too little to understand what was happening, who these people were, why I was living with them, why I was playing with someone else's toys, all that.

I kept having nightmares too. I did for years. Even now, sometimes. In the nightmares Dad is coming to kill me. I'd be screaming and crying and scared in the middle of the night.

Eventually I found the Lord and that has made me feel much better.

I had so much pent-up anger and I didn't know what to do with it. I hit my foster mother. She said, "If you hit me again you won't be able to stay here." But I didn't know how to stop myself. They put me in therapy for ADHD and that helped me focus but it didn't make the pain go away.

So I had to leave that foster home and those kind people.

Every foster home after that, I ended up in restraints. I was a really angry kid. The Children's Aid got to the end of their list of people who would take me so I got sent to a group home. I wasn't beaten there but I ended up in restraints almost every day.

I guess every group home is different. This one had a level system. Level Five was the highest. At Level Five you got two hours of TV time and you got to go on outings. It took me a long time to get to Level Five. Usually I had early bedtime, no TV, no outings, nothing.

Just down the street from this all-boys group home was a penitentiary. The group home staff would sometimes say, "There's your next home, guys," and they'd laugh.

This group home was literally hell, worse than any place I'd been. It was full of kids like me that no foster parents wanted, kids that knew no one wanted them. It was supposed to be a therapy place but we were all too angry and messed up to receive therapy. We learned how to control our behavior to get along there, and I guess that's therapy, but nothing got fixed. We knew what everyone thought of us. We could tell from the condition of the place that we weren't wanted. It was a dump. Mold, even. It felt like the whole world was against us.

When I was fifteen they moved me out of the group home and into another foster home. There was another foster kid there who was my age. He used to beat me up all the time to "make me tougher." The foster parents didn't notice or they pretended not to notice, and I sure didn't tell.

Another kid moved in. Remember, I was trying hard not to fight. I was trying hard to change myself because I felt God wanted me to do better. This new kid moved in and he had an Airsoft gun. He shot me so many times! He threatened to kill me and burn up my body. It was just awful. I wanted to die.

Finally I told somebody at my school. They called Children's Aid and I got moved to a new home.

In this new home I wasn't hit but I was treated like

nothing, like I didn't matter. I didn't last long there because they didn't like me and I didn't like them.

Now I wonder if they hated me because I'm gay. They never said so and I didn't really know myself well enough to be able to define myself, but maybe they knew before I did and hated me because they just hated gays. I'll never know, but I'll always remember what it felt like to have to live with people who did not want me there. You just feel like nothing.

Because of my anger I've had the cops called on me many times. They charge me with creating a disturbance or assault or they just come and remove me for a bit to calm me down or they give me a warning.

I did get arrested for theft once. I was high on pot at the time and they charged me with a few things. I had to go through the courts. They put me into a diversion program, which ended up being a course I had to take to help me realize why I did it and that it was not smart.

I can't say that the program changed everything for me, but it did give me a place to start thinking more seriously about my life.

After the foster home where they were so cold to me and hoped I'd go away, I got put into another one where I got constantly treated like crap. When I tried to defend myself, they called the cops. My foster mom said my anger was so bad she was scared for her child. I said, "Do you think I'm going to kill your child?" But what she heard was "I'm going to kill your child." So she called the cops.

The cops didn't charge me. For once they believed me. All they did was take me out of the home.

They put me in another foster home and I was there until I aged out.

I've been seeing a therapist lately. He said I should imagine a stove top and put Dad and all the pain into a pot on the back burner and put a tight lid on the pot. That way I know where all those memories and feelings are and that they are contained and I don't have to deal with them all

?

• What makes you angry? How does anger feel? How do you respond to these feelings? Has your anger gotten you in trouble? How do you feel when someone around you is angry? Can anger ever be a positive thing?

the time. I can put myself and what I want to become on the front burner.

I'm figuring out now that this is the only way. I'm a lot stronger today than ever. I'm even happy now.

My father's actions influence me to be the same as him. I'm going to break those chains free. I forgive him. I don't like him. He was beaten himself when he was young, and he also went through the system. You don't have to have your father's love to be loved. You don't have to have his love to be able to love someone else.

All these adults in my life that were paid to look after me. Some of them really cared and kept me going. I could not understand why they cared so much about me. A lot of others did not care, but some cared about me even when I could not care about myself. That's probably why I'm still here today.

It's hard to help someone who doesn't want help at the time, but if someone could have explained to me the psychology of what it's like to recover from beatings and abuse, then maybe I'd have been a little better able to understand and handle what I was feeling.

It would also have helped if the Children's Aid had been more open with me about what they were doing with me and why. Like all the ADHD tests they gave me, all the meds they put me on, all the places they moved me to then took me out of. I would have liked a lot more consultation about my life.

Now I'm over eighteen and no longer part of Children's Aid. I have a small check from them every month that goes directly to my landlord for rent with a bit of money left over for me. I don't have a job yet. I completed grade ten but then dropped out because I couldn't focus. My dream career is acting and books can't teach you that.

I've constantly lived with different faces, hiding myself from people in order to get along. I've blocked my emotions. I'm good at hiding how I feel. To survive in all the situations I got in, I had to put on different faces.

When I finally came out gay, it was scary telling people

who I am, but being gay is who I am and hiding it from myself and everybody else isn't going to work anymore.

I want to tell young people who are going through the same thing as me: You are not alone. If you're being bullied, if you're afraid, reach out and talk to someone. It will make you feel powerful and more like who you really are.

Your secrets don't protect you. They protect the ones who are beating you.

Taking Steps ...

For yourself

The next time you get angry, take a step outside yourself and look at what's going on in your body and your mind. Take some deep breaths to calm yourself down. Does that help you to feel better and think more clearly?

For others

If you know a teacher or other adult who has a bad temper, look for a safe way to tell them how it makes you feel. If it's a teacher, perhaps you and a classmate could write them a polite letter, keeping a copy of it for yourselves.

Voice of Experience: Seth, 43*

On the day of my birth my mom was seventeen years old with a grade-six education and my father was an alcoholic drug addict who took off pretty much out the gate. Maybe a handful of visits until I was four. Shortly after, my mom met my sister's father and married and ten months after I was born, my mom was pregnant again.

My sister's father was a complete terror. The very first years of my life were violence and abuse. This man shot me in the back with an air power pellet gun when I was four. He used to throw me in the chicken coop and then throw birdfeed on me so the chickens would peck me. He burned my toys on the barbecue.

My whole family was afraid of this guy. We moved to a different part of the country to get away from him.

My family was poor and uneducated. We stayed with my aunt and her three kids. Somehow my sister's dad found us. My sister and me were playing in the yard. I looked up to see arms pick my sister up. He threw my sister in his car and drove away. It took Mom years to get her back. She had to go back to our first province to get her. She left me with my aunt, who had horses and she'd whip us kids with the horse strap. She made me drink Suave shampoo until I threw up and then she hit me for throwing up. There was sexual abuse, too, from a male relative. He said if he didn't let me do what he wanted, he'd tell my aunt and then she would beat me.

My grandma sensed something was wrong with me and she pulled me out of this house and let me live with her until my mom came back. I only felt safe with my grandma and now my wife.

My mom finally came back with my sister and a new husband, just another man who treated me poorly. When I was twelve, he kicked me out of the house.

I was a small kid growing up in a rough neighborhood. I knew my mom loved me, but at the time I felt some animosity over her not sticking up for me. I never understood until years later that she was immobilized by her

* Text sent in a letter written in prison

own fear, and with only a grade-six education, she probably felt trapped.

At the age of eight I started doing B and E's. My uncle put me through a basement window and told me to open the door for him, that it was his buddy's house. After doing this at multiple houses, I realized what was going on. So I started to do the break-ins on my own, only I never looked for money or jewelry. I only did it to eat food and I stole toys. When I did take money, it was only quarters and pocket change.

I know the exact point in my life that I made the choice to go down this road. It was just before my twelfth birthday. Teenagers held me down and spraypainted my face with orange paint. A few days later I was with some of my friends skateboarding, and I saw one of the teens that painted me. I got my friends to go with me and beat that kid. He was standing around the corner at this 7-Eleven and I came around behind him and smashed his head in with my skateboard. My friends and I put a beating on that kid that would make him never beat on anyone again.

It was in that moment that I realized all the abuse, which was my whole life, was nothing I could control, but from this point on, no one would ever put their hands on me again.

I started going to the young offenders court at age twelve. My criminal record is as long as a skyscraper is tall, from simple theft to first-degree murder. From the ages of twelve to nineteen, I was only on the streets for a total of six months. The rest of the time I was in custody.

Now I'm in prison with a mandatory life sentence, which in Canada is twenty-five years. I have the same basic story as a lot of the souls behind these walls, a life filled with violence, sexual abuse, neglect, poverty and fear of being hurt emotionally, physically and sexually, fear of abandonment, fear of not being loved, fear of not being worthy of being loved or cared for.

For a lot of years, I blamed myself for the abuse and abandonment. It wasn't until I met my wife that I opened up and she helped me realize it wasn't my fault. I do deserve to be loved.

I am now forty-three years old and twenty years into my life sentence. I never even started to acknowledge the things that happened to me until the last four years. I buried it all so far down that it was shocking when it started to surface.

I've been repeatedly stabbed in prison. Once I actually died in here from being attacked by another inmate. They brought me back to life. I've spent over 1300 days in segregation. I now spend every second of my life with someone else controlling my day. I can't figure out how I was ever content with this, how I wanted to die like a gangster! Tragic is what that is.

Despite all these wasted years, I still breathe in air and there still can be life for me outside these walls.

It's such a shame that we can't figure out how to divert our youth from all this shit. All our youth facilities are is a breeding ground for more killers, crooks and gangsters.

I hope to go home one day and give some of my time and experience to help kids who grew up as I did.

Just know that this lifestyle, these streets, don't give back to you. They just take from you. It's always a one-way relationship.

Beth, 19

"That little thing that's in the back of your head that says, 'Don't do this!'? Listen to it the first time."

Punitive justice seeks to punish the offender. Restorative justice seeks to fix the harm that was done and restore the offender to responsible, full participation in society. Much of it based on Indigenous teachings from around the world, restorative justice is a process where the offender can own up to what they have done, make restitution, seek forgiveness and then move on with their lives. Some young offenders may qualify for diversion programs, an alternative way of holding someone accountable without increasing the burden on the courts and jails. It is a way for victims to be able to have a say in what the offender could do to repair some of the damage they did.

Diversion programs are often based on the restorative-justice model, which focuses on addressing the harm caused, holding the offender responsible for their actions and providing the parties directly affected (including the victims, offenders, families and communities) with a forum to identify and address their needs in repairing the harm and, if possible, restoring relationships.

I had never been in trouble before. Never.
    This all happened when I was sixteen. There was a group of us friends out together, driving around the back roads. I had my camera with me—I was into

?

- Why is it hard for us to admit when we make mistakes?
- Have you ever been in a situation where things got out of hand? How might you have handled it differently?

photography—and we drove by this abandoned factory that I thought would make for some good pictures.

There were No Trespassing signs posted but we ignored them and went inside one of the back doors. It was really cool-looking inside, like a movie set, with random bits of machinery and things like old safety posters, a work glove, bits of people's personal things, old work benches, things like that.

We got inside and I realized I'd left my camera back in the car, so the whole point of being in there wasn't there anymore, but we didn't leave. We all had our phones on us and took some pictures that way, but it wasn't what I'd wanted to do. If all we did was break in and look around, it still wouldn't be right, but it wouldn't have been that bad.

But things got out of hand. No, *we* got out of hand. My friends went a little crazy. They picked up these old fire extinguishers and started setting them off inside the building.

I was yelling, "Someone's going to see us!" because we were in front of these big windows that faced the road. But, you know, you get caught up in the fun of the moment. I also didn't want to be the only one standing around not doing anything, not having fun.

We did our thing and then left the factory and went on with our lives, no problem.

The town was upset, though. The factory had been an employer in the town for generations. It was part of the town's history, part of its heart and soul. Nearly every family had some sort of connection to the place, and when people learned there had been damage done in it, they were upset.

Still, I thought we were home free. I even really forgot about it.

Then, a month after we did it, I was waiting to get on the school bus to come home when I got a call from my mom. She said the police had called her and she had to take me to the police station as soon as I got home.

It was not a good feeling.

Mom and I had to sit in a tiny interrogation room with an officer. I remember there was a stupid little cockroach in the room. It was right down by my foot. I kept looking at it and wondering how it got there.

Before we talked to the officer we talked with a lawyer but it became pretty clear pretty quickly that they had me. The police had us all on footage from a surveillance camera across the road from the factory. Plus, one of my friends posted a photo of us in the factory on social media, and the police had printed that out, so there was no point in denying that I did it. Not only did they have my picture, they had my picture wearing the exact same jacket and scarf I had on in the interrogation room!

I was formally charged with break and enter and with mischief under $5000.

We were all kept separate, my friends and I, and we weren't allowed to have any contact with each other until it was all over. I was in a relationship with one of them, so that put an end to that.

It all took a lot of time. Getting arrested takes up a lot of time! A lot of waiting around, being bored and scared, and changing your life around to make court dates. I had to go to court three times. The first time was in February. It was the first day of the second semester and I had to miss school to go to court. Also, I had to change one of my courses because one of the girls I broke into the factory with was in that class and I wasn't allowed to be around her.

Court was awful. I was so scared. There was a girl right behind me shackled right up! All the defendants were young, like me. The judge was kind of rude. I didn't know when to stand or sit and he kind of yelled at me for that.

I was let into a diversion program. This was a way of avoiding having a criminal record. I had to go in front of this committee and talk to them about what I did. I had to explain my intentions in going into the factory. The friends I went into the factory with were not with me at the meeting. I had to stand before the committee by myself and explain what I had done and why. The committee then got to decide what was going to happen to me.

One of the things I had to do was to write a letter of apology to the woman who was the caretaker of the factory. This woman then had all of us meet her for a tour of a museum about the history of the factory.

It was during that tour that I realized what I had done. I knew it was stupid but until then I only thought about how my stupidity affected me. During the tour I realized that we had disrespected the memories of all the people who had worked there. We could have damaged things that were part of the town's history, things that could never be replaced.

The whole thing—getting arrested, going to court, going through the diversion program—it all made me super conscious of every move I made, not to make a stupid move again. I know I came really close to maybe not ruining my life but certainly doing it a lot of damage. I had to answer to all these people, and it made me really think about what I'd done.

My mom was one hundred percent disappointed in me. She was not pleased to have to take time off work to drive

Taking Steps ...

For yourself

Have you ever hurt anyone in a way that you can make up for now? Can you apologize and fix what was broken?

Have you ever been hurt by someone? If that person won't make amends, how can you look after yourself so you don't carry the hurt with you?

For others

Find something damaged that can be restored and gather friends to restore it with you — clean a playground or pull weeds for someone who can't do it themselves.

If you know of a family that has lost things in a fire, find a way to help them out.

me to court and everything, but she stood by me and got me through it. I never want to disappoint her like that again. The rest of my family, my relatives, don't know anything about it. It's just embarrassing to me that I got myself into that mess.

Two pieces of advice: That little thing that's in the back of your head that says, "Don't do this!"? Listen to it the first time.

And when you make a mistake, learn from it. And then move on.

Voice of Experience: Marina, Diversion Worker

The diversion program gives youth who are first-time offenders an opportunity to recognize their behavior and address it in a different manner. It can help youth understand what they did to themselves and to their community.

We do take repeat offenders, too, as long as the youth are willing to continue to engage with the program. Sometimes they are more ready for it the second time around. They will often say they probably should have listened more the first time!

A common thing we see are youth with mental health problems that have not yet been diagnosed or addressed. We see struggles like anxiety, depression, trouble in families. Youth often won't admit to their struggles and parents might not believe their son or daughter has these issues.

Our mental health system still requires labels. Youth sometimes just need someone to talk to who is strictly on their side, but counselors often can't be accessed without a diagnosis.

Also, youth have to volunteer to participate in treatment. One of the myths out there is that the court system can "fix" someone, force them into treatment, but that's not the case. If a youth is sentenced to custody, they may be offered a treatment option, but if they refuse, they go into ordinary custody.

When there are complex things going on in their minds and their lives, the youth might not recognize they need help until they have been receiving it for a while, until they have a sense they can trust those counseling them. The court system cannot impose treatment. They can put forward recommendations, but that's it.

Youth entering the diversion program have to be willing to admit their wrong-doing.

They can go before a committee of community members

Restorative justice is a process that brings together the offender, the victim, their supporters and interested people in the community. It requires the offender to admit they did the offense, to hear the impact of the offense on the victim, and to take steps to assure the victim they won't do it again, to anyone. They also have to fix what they broke — make restitution to the victim and to the community.

It can be a way for all involved to have their voices heard. The victim can have a say in what the restitution should be. The offender can fully understand the impact of their actions and take steps to learn why they acted that way. The offender's subsequent contribution to the victim and the community can build their sense of self-worth and belonging.

In Indigenous communities, healing circles have long been a way to repair the damage caused by someone hurting someone else.

Restorative justice has been part of the Canadian legal system for more than forty years. It "focuses on addressing the harm caused by the crime while holding the offender responsible for their actions, by providing an opportunity for the parties directly affected by the crime — victims, offenders and communities — to identify and address their needs in the aftermath of a crime. ... Restorative justice is based on an understanding that crime is a violation of people and relationships. The principles of restorative justice are based on respect, compassion and inclusivity. Restorative justice encourages meaningful engagement and accountability and provides an opportunity for healing, reparation and reintegration." (A Little Manual of Restorative Justice)

Different forms of restorative justice are practiced in countries around the world. The third week of November each year is designated International Restorative Justice Week.

who volunteer for the job. The staff and the committee spend a lot of time on case management, looking at school, family and so on, not just on the offense.

The program is most successful when the plans we and the youth come up with are meaningful to them. The committee wants to get to know the youth, what they've been up to, and what's really going on in their lives.

The most powerful part of the process, I've found, is when youth hear the impact of their actions on the victims. The success rate is much higher when they hear directly from the person they have hurt.

If the youth does not complete the plan they have agreed to, they get referred back to the police and the regular court system.

In the regular justice system, there's a push to "Don't talk to anybody about what you have done." It encourages people to build a story where the offender has done nothing wrong. They work on that story leading up to court and that story becomes their truth. They begin to believe that's what happened. The regular justice system is about trying to get away with things.

In diversion, you admit that you've done something wrong, now let's try to understand why and make amends. Humans have to be accountable for their actions, even young humans. When they learn to care about their community and take responsibility for what occurred, then they can learn to do things differently in the future.

We still have a society that wants punishment, retaliation and retribution. Custody centers are good at keeping people in one space, but not good at rehabilitation.

It's hard to sell society and politicians on prevention. You can say a lot about how much money we'll save when we invest in youth before they commit a crime, versus how much it will cost us to keep them in jail, but there isn't one thing we can point to and definitely say, "This is the answer."

Because there isn't just one thing. There are many. In diversion we understand that each youth is an individual.

They can learn that there are caring adults in the world that they can trust. They learn that there are people they can go to and ask for help before they get into trouble again.

Leon, 18

"When I was sixteen I wanted to join a gang because then I'd always have friends who would watch out for me."

Unlike other groups, gangs act outside the law to gain power. Youth can be drawn to gangs for protection (often from threats by rival gangs), for excitement, for the promise of wealth, for friendship. Some gangs promote racist ideologies. Others are organized along national or cultural identities, or around neighborhoods. There can be gang colors, gang graffiti, gang tattoos and gang hand gestures — all ways to show whether someone is in the club or not. Some gangs form as a response to feeling powerless. Its members were never going to be accepted by mainstream society, never going to rise above others' prejudice toward them, and gang activity is about sticking it to those with real power — the police, the courts, the banks, the politicians.

Gang activity includes violence. "The average death rate for African Americans fourteen to seventeen years of age is 1 in 1000 a year; if they join the gang it is 1 in 80." (Richard Swift, *Gangs*, 50). Gang life also leads to injuries, arrests and prison time. It is not a glamorous life, but opportunities in the legitimate world are often so limited that many see gangs as the only viable economic alternative, even with the risks.

I was born on one side of the country and raised on the other side of the country. My mother took me from where I started and brought me to this province.

I put myself in foster care.

My mom had a boyfriend who was abusive—sexually, physically and verbally. The Children's Aid was always involved with us, but when they came to check on me, Mom would say, "Everything is good, my son is in school, he goes every day." The boyfriend would be out when the worker came by and the worker just took Mom's word.

Mom wouldn't let me use the phone. She'd yell, "You're not calling that damn worker!"

So I'd call the worker from school. I kept on calling until they did something. I was eight at the time.

They put me into a foster home. I got kicked out of there because they said I ate food from the kitchen that they'd put aside for something else, I forget what it was. I didn't eat that food but they wouldn't believe me and they kicked me out.

I tried living with Mom again after she got rid of that boyfriend. For a year or two it was okay. Not great. Okay.

When I was twelve I got a job selling chocolate bars and I was so successful at it! I sold and sold and sold and sold, door to door, on the street, anywhere. I made thousands of dollars selling chocolate bars.

I wish I had some of that money now. Mom stole a lot of it. She needed it for rent or drugs or booze or smokes or to give to her new boyfriend. Sometimes she'd say, "Give it here, I'll pay you back," but we both knew she never would. The rest I spent on stupid stuff, like I'd buy things for others so they'd be impressed with me. It all went away pretty fast.

I went in and out of foster care. When I got to be too much trouble at home, Mom would call the worker and say, "Take him, I can't handle him." Or I would call and say, "She's getting bad again. I need a place." Then Mom would miss the extra money she gets from me living with her and she'd call Children's Aid and tell them she was doing great and she wanted me back.

Some of the foster homes were all right. The third one was awesome. The foster dad there taught me how to barbecue and he'd let me do the whole dinner once I got the hang of it.

Each time I went back to Mom in the beginning I was hopeful it would be okay. After it wasn't, over and over, I always had a wall up with her. I was always waiting for her to send it all south and she always did.

Doesn't mean I didn't try. I would try. I'd do things for her around the house, like do the cleaning, do the laundry, wash the dishes, sometimes make the meals. She sometimes was nice about it but then she'd just be rude. It was always wrong, what I was doing. One time she grabbed my arm and twisted it until I was on the ground. My wrist is still injured from that. I don't know why she did it, why she had to be like that.

When I was sixteen I wanted to join a gang because then I'd always have friends who would watch out for me and who I could hang out with.

To get into a gang you have to do an initiation, some job or challenge that they dream up and make you do to see if you're tough enough for them, to make sure you're not someone who will turn on them. They set me the task of masked robbery of a convenience store.

At first, when I headed to the shop and when I went inside and started the robbery, the energy was flowing and it was great. But then I saw a girl leaving the store—running away, scared—and I felt bad. I hadn't thought about scaring people. I only thought about proving myself to the gang.

I guess that girl called the police or the store owner pressed an alarm button because the police came and they got me. They charged me with masked robbery. They said they would have charged me with armed robbery but they couldn't find a weapon. I told them I didn't have a weapon. That's the truth, but they didn't believe me.

I did three months locked up for that. I served it at a youth reformatory up north. I'm a little surprised I didn't get longer. While I was in the reformatory I tried to kill myself so they shipped me to a big detention center in a city and threw me in the hole for a week so they could watch me.

That gang I did all this for decided I wasn't tough enough for them or a good enough thief or whatever and they kicked me out. I heard this while I was in the reformatory. So I had no one. No one.

When I got out of jail I decided to make my own gang, a helping gang, a gang that was dedicated to only doing good things and helping people who were hurting or scared. I even had the colors picked out—pink and white. When someone in the gang saw a pink and white bandana on someone else, they'd know they were part of the same gang and they could join together to do some good.

I still think that's a good idea. I'll probably end up doing it when I get myself straightened around.

When I was seventeen I was charged with theft under $5000 and mischief under $5000. I was at a shelter and they said they had a personal needs check for me, a benefits check, but they wouldn't give it to me when I wanted it. I was too drunk to listen to the reason and I smashed a window and I guess I stole something. I can't really remember that part.

The charges on that were later dropped but I can't ever go back to that shelter. I can't really blame them.

I have a daughter. She's a year old now. She was born on Canada Day, so I say that the fireworks on that day are really for her. I don't get to see her at the moment, but

- What do you think of the idea of a "helping gang"? Would you like to belong to that sort of a gang?
- Leon bought things for other people so they would be impressed with him. Have you ever done something like that? What are other ways we can impress people while still being true to ourselves?

Taking Steps ...

For yourself

Leon had to call the social worker to get help for himself. He was his own advocate. What is something you can advocate for yourself to get (help with chemistry, a stop sign on a busy street you have to cross, proper gym equipment)?

For others

What is a secret way you or you and your friends can do good for someone else, either an individual or the larger community?

once I get things going in the right way, that could change. I want to do good for her.

The things I like to do are sports—football, basketball, table tennis, all sports. I like dancing, rapping and singing too.

I'd like to train for some kind of technical job, mechanics or computers. I like concentrating on small details. I feel calm when I do that. The rest of the world goes away. I'd like to play music too. I taught myself how to play the flute.

I'd like to spend my life with a really good woman, one who knows herself really well and is strong and who will make me want to have a good life, even if it isn't always easy.

Voice of Experience: Ken, 69

My parents didn't give a damn what I did. The only time period they weren't totally indifferent to me was when I was a rising hockey star. Then they paid attention. When the hockey ended, they went back to ignoring me.

My parents fought all the time, inside and outside the house. All the kids I hung around with saw it and heard it. Maybe their parents fought too. We never talked about it. I remember hating being at home because of the fighting and I'd stay away as much as I could.

We formed ourselves into gangs, even in elementary school. I remember being tied to a tree and getting beat up by a rival gang. I was ten or eleven.

My parents were working class but wanted to move up to middle class. That's why they brought us to the suburbs. My dad drove a taxi then later went into kitchen appliance sales with his brothers. They had a big store and made a lot of money, but that was after I was in high school.

When we first moved to the suburbs of this big city, most of the area was still under construction. The gangs and I would do so much destruction with these sites, breaking things, stealing stuff. We never thought about the consequences. We just thought about the adventure.

We stole a lot of stuff! We had a system of stealing from stores. We'd use lookouts and distract the owners. We stole mostly food and clothes or shoes. Stuff we knew kids needed. Many of our gang lived in public housing, so we'd steal stuff and give it away. You didn't eat yesterday because your old man drank the grocery money? We'll steal some bread and salami for you. Your shoes fell apart? We'll steal you new ones. It was better than stealing for ourselves. It gave us a sense of purpose, like we were good people, Robin Hoods, sticking it to the rich.

There was one really terrible thing we did, such a stupid thing. We'd stand by the highway and throw rocks at car windows. Once we broke a window on a transport truck. We ran back to our meeting place to celebrate. We were all bragging together about how many cars we hit. I turned around and there was the driver of the transport truck. He'd tracked us down.

We all went silent and he lit into us! "You could have killed somebody!" he yelled. I remember him being surprised at how stupid we were. It was the first time in my life I ever thought about the consequences. I remember being impressed that this guy took the time to track us down and bawl us out and call the cops. It's like he was saying, "It's important to me that you smarten up!" I hated having the cops called on us but there was also the message that he thought I was valuable enough to be mad at.

So many times in and out of court. I never felt ashamed. I remember the system trying to make me feel ashamed. I remember standing with my mom in court and thinking, *When is this going to be over so I can go back to my buddies?* I remember my mom being annoyed that I was causing trouble for her, but neither of my parents were surprised when I was arrested. I don't think they thought I was worth much else.

The community of guys, my friends, my gang, was for

me a safe way to get out of the house. I never had any friends come back to my home because I never knew what my parents might do or what shape they'd be in. As long as I stayed out of their sight, my parents didn't care where I was. I'd be out all night. We'd break into some apartment complex's pool at 4 a.m. and go for a swim and my parents didn't care.

A lot of the kids I grew up with in that gang are now dead or in prison. I've always felt on the outside of things, and I think that's what saved me. I knew a life of crime wasn't for me because I knew it would lead to jail and I wasn't interested in that. Also, I never wanted to hurt people.

I was a great hockey player. Even as a kid I could shoot the puck one hundred miles per hour. Coaches would try to get me to shoot the puck at the goalie's head. Violence at home. Violence in the street. Violence on the ice. I was scouted by major leagues and put into their system. In those days, there were fewer major league teams, and they would put possible players under contract early. I remember my parents signing something with one of the teams and the team rep turning to me and saying, "Now we own you, kid." But I didn't really feel like hockey was for me either. One of the country's top coaches saw me play and said, "This is one of the best players I've ever seen but I've also never seen a young man less willing to hurt people."

I knew that if I was ever going to find a life for myself, one that didn't involve violence, that I was going to have to make it happen. No one would do it for me. I put myself through university by delivering appliances for my dad all over the province, lifting fridges in and out of people's homes. Got my BA, then decided I wanted to study theology, so I got a Master's degree in that.

You see, the world was giving me something bigger to do, bigger than violence. Bigger than hockey. I grew up watching the civil rights protesters being attacked by police dogs, anti-war students shot by National Guard soldiers. All around, people were standing up for justice. I started working on the grape boycott to support farmworkers in California. My life has been spent on non-violent direct action for the rights of people to live without war or oppression.

As an adult I've been arrested dozens of times—for sitting down in front of the war department, for non-violent actions against nuclear power plants, the arms race and torture. I've been beaten by police and by people who feel powerful when they hurt others. As a result of all those beatings, I'm now confined in a wheelchair and live in an assisted-living home. But this past May I organized the first-ever gay pride rally in my small town. Three hundred people came out.

For all the violence and crap and disappointment and abuse you are living through, you can still emerge with something strong—your sense of who you are and what you believe. Do not let anyone define that for you—and believe me, others will try. Your self belongs to you. You've got to find out who you are and hold onto it.

It's not easy though. Abuse comes back again, even years later. All I have to do is see a little kid about the age I was when my parents started beating me and I start to cry. After all these years.

Stuart, 19

"I had to change my whole story about myself."

In 1932, amphetamines were put into nose sprays for people suffering from asthma. During World War II, pilots took amphetamines to stay awake. In the 1950s, people used them legally to stay up for long hours. When the health dangers became clear in the 1960s and 1970s, legal production ended and illegal production and trade took over.

Crystal meth, Stuart's drug of choice, is one of the most addictive of the illegal drugs. Your body can become dependent on it in a very short time, and increasing amounts are needed to satisfy the craving.

Crystal meth is made, in part, with battery acid and drain cleaner. It can cause brain damage, heart damage, convulsions and death.

I was born in Canada but moved to Austria when I was three, and then moved back to Canada when I was seventeen.

My parents split up when I was little. My mom met a guy online and moved me to Austria so we could live with him. In Austria it is normal for me, and calm. I went to school, did normal things. I got my high-school diploma by the time I was fifteen. I started a chef apprenticeship there after high school. Then Mom's relationship ended and we moved back to Canada.

It was great being in Austria. We traveled all around Europe. The other countries are so close over there. Paris and Rome are my favorite cities. I can speak German, English and a good bit of French.

I have two and a half sisters. Two are from when Mom and Dad were together and the half is from her relationship in Austria.

> "Everything is story. I am story. You are story. The universe is story. I am all the things that I tell myself .... We can decide which story we want to be in and tell it to ourselves ..."
> — Harold R. Johnson, *Firewater: How Alcohol Is Killing My People (and Yours)*

Just after I moved back here I learned that my girlfriend in Austria of six years had killed herself. I couldn't handle it. I didn't know what to do. Maybe if I hadn't have come back to Canada she wouldn't have done it. I felt so bad. A friend said, "Here, take this, it will take the edge off." So I took what he gave me.

It was crystal meth. I became addicted to it in, like, no time.

Crystal meth is bad stuff. It makes your face break out in huge acne and it makes you feel like you've got bugs crawling under your skin so you claw at your face and you look really horrible.

I don't take it anymore. I got myself off it. I stopped a year ago, just through willpower. I wouldn't recommend that! I got really, really sick.

Taking that first hit of crystal meth was the start of it. Since then I've had marijuana charges and assault charges.

The marijuana charge came because my buddies and I were really stupid. It was St. Patrick's Day. I got a call and they said, "Come meet us around the corner," so I did. Just as I rounded the corner, I could see them standing there smoking this two-foot bong, and just as I got to them, two police cruisers pulled over behind us. I had stuff on me, too, so we all got arrested.

I went through a diversion program. I had to take a John Howard course about drugs and the law and healthy living. It was all right. I learned things there.

The assault charge came at school.

I should back up. I found out that graduating high school in Austria is not the same as graduating high school here in Canada. I applied for college—culinary school—and was told I needed a Canadian educational assessment, and when that came back, I was told I needed to go back to high school to get a few more credits, including three courses that I really do not like — English, math and chemistry.

I thought I was done with high school. I'd been really proud of myself because I was a kid who had finished high school at fifteen and that seemed like such a big deal to have done that. When I came back here and found out I wasn't finished, I had to change my whole story about myself. I wasn't such a big deal after all.

I wasn't happy about it, but I enrolled back in school.

The assault charge happened because this guy—used to be a buddy of mine, actually—he was sexually harassing a former girlfriend of mine. He was constantly at her in school. He wouldn't stop. I think he did it as much to get to me as he did to get to her because he saw how much it bothered me.

One day I got so mad at him I blacked out with rage. I broke a chair and attacked him. Half the class had to restrain me.

The rage blackout could have been an effect of the drugs, even though I had quit crystal meth by then. That stuff messes with your brain for a long time.

I'll find out in a month what's going to happen with my assault charge. I was supposed to go to court with it over the summer but the court date fell on Mom's wedding day. She's getting married again, to the guy who fathered her latest kid. I'm going to have another sibling. Another half. Mom's new boyfriend doesn't like me so I stay away from that situation.

My dad beat up his girlfriend when she was eight and a half months pregnant. I don't know if I've got that sort of mean in me or not. I hope I don't. I believe strongly that men should never lay a hand on a woman when they're angry, and I hope I stick to that.

Now I'm homeless and looking for a shelter bed. I go to youth centers and community centers to get something to eat. It helps so much that these places are there, and I'll keep going until I can get some money and do some things to get on my feet.

My hope for the future? That I can come out of this struggle and better myself. I'd like to go to college to learn how to make video games and eventually I'd like to run a music studio. I'm done with cooking school. Something else will fit me better. I'll finish my last high-school credit soon.

Music is my safe place when I'm down and sliding into depression. I play guitar, drums and piano. Of course, now that I'm homeless, I'm not doing those things, although one of the community centers where I sometimes eat has a piano that I can play to entertain people.

My advice to others in my situation would be, number one—Don't take that first hit of crystal meth. Seriously! You don't want to do that! It will mess you up a hundred times worse than you think you're messed up right now.

The second advice I'd give you would be to stay in school. Don't throw away your life. If you leave school before you finish, you'll only have to go back again to do pretty much anything you'll want to do and going back once you've been out is just a major pain.

Don't mess up your life. Listen to your parents if they

?

- Stuart's father was a violent man. How can Stuart avoid becoming violent?
- Stuart lost his girl-friend to suicide and turned to drugs to escape the pain. Have you ever experienced terrible grief, or do you know someone who has? How can people cope with grief without using booze or drugs?

Taking Steps ...

For yourself

Research how different cultures, including your own, deal with grief. Think about what you might need if you ever lose someone you love.

For others

Spread the news about what drugs like crystal meth can do to your body and your brain. Make posters and put them around the school. Prepare an infomercial and broadcast it over the school's public address system during morning announcements.

make any sense at all. Stay strong. Don't take the easy
way out. There are other ways to get through things
besides taking your own life. Hang on, stay strong, get
through the bad
moment and there's
a good chance that
life will get better
for you.

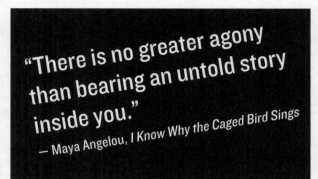

"There is no greater agony
than bearing an untold story
inside you."
— Maya Angelou, *I Know Why the Caged Bird Sings*

I've saved eight
kids from suicide,
talked them out of
taking their own
lives when they were right on the edge of doing it. I've told
them they can always find a reason to keep going.

Now I just have to find my own reason. Someone told me
once that God loves me. I wonder why.

Garnett, 18

"Nobody would ask me. Not really. The worker would maybe ask, 'How's it going?' and I'd say fine because what else was I going to say? That's what kids say when you ask them that question."

During World War II, the Nazis put people they didn't like into concentration camps, killing millions of them. For those who survived, their pain did not end when the war was over. They carried that trauma with them, and their children were affected by it. This is called generational trauma.

Indigenous peoples have been traumatized and retraumatized over and over. Forced relocation. Abuse at residential schools. Children taken from parents and put into white foster homes. Ignorant government policies. Police who have too often seen every Indigenous person as a potential criminal. It all adds up to a huge overrepresentation of First Nations, Métis and Inuit people in jail. Aboriginal youth make up 6 percent of Canada's young people, but 44 percent of the population of young people in prison (www.prisonjustice.ca).

I've lived everywhere. My parents are Mohawk and Ojibwe. I've never lived on a reserve but I've lived close to them.

I came into Children's Aid care when I was really young. My parents were alcoholics. Dad was abusive and Mom was depressed, so they couldn't take care of a baby.

I've been in fifteen or sixteen foster homes and group homes.

I found it all so frustrating and confusing, going from place to place. I started acting out. My authority figures changed all the time so I thought, "Screw authority."

Most of the time no one would tell me what was going on when a change was happening. Once I woke up and the foster mom was in my room, packing up my stuff. She said, "Hurry up! Get dressed! Your worker will be here any minute!"

Nobody would ask me. Not really. The worker would maybe ask, "How's it going?" and I'd say fine because what else was I going to say? That's what kids say when you ask them that question.

I wonder what all those families thought when they closed the door on me. I guess they were happy to see me go. Maybe they never gave me another thought.

At first when I'd get into a new home I'd be anxious because everything was new. I got used to the routine of it. First you do intake—have a tour of the place, listen to the plan of care, meet the other kids in the house, get the rules, all that. I got used to that part, but I never got over being anxious about it. I got tired of being anxious but I never got over it.

When I'd meet the new kids in a new house, whether it's a group home or a foster home, they'd always test me to see what they could get away with, and I didn't like to be tested. They'd try to go through my things or take my things or say, "You can't use this bathroom, you have to

> "To shut up a child in a dimly-lit cell, for twenty-three hours out of the twenty-four, is an example of the cruelty of stupidity. If an individual, parent or guardian, did this to a child, he would be severely punished ... The inhuman treatment of a child is always inhuman, by whomsoever it is inflicted. But inhuman treatment by Society is to the child the more terrible because there is no appeal."
>
> — Oscar Wilde (after serving two years in prison and seeing the treatment of the children held there), *Children in Prison and Other Cruelties of Prison Life*, 1897

pee outside." Or they'd steal something, break something, and blame it on me.

I had to fight back right away or that would just continue the whole time I was there. I knew I'd be tested every time I got moved. I just never knew what the test would look like in each new place.

When you look at the world like that, even if people are nice to you, you don't trust what they're saying. If people were friendly, I'd pick fights just to get the tension inside me over with.

I never got placed in a Native foster home, not once. Always white. I had no chance to learn about my culture until I was fourteen. An aunt took me to live with her on a reserve. There wasn't much there. I fell into the life-style easily. I got involved with bad stuff. Not much else to do, or if there was I was too wound up to do it. I got involved with the gang culture on the reserve. A lot of the Aboriginal gangs are mixed up with the Hells Angels, so that's heavy stuff.

I got bigger and got into more trouble—assaults, fights, charges like assault with a weapon. I began to be the kid who tested the new kids who came into the group home. I stole a lot of cars, did a lot of dangerous behaviors. I ended up burning a kid's face with an aerosol and a lighter.

Why? Why did I do that? I don't remember why. No good reason. Is there ever a good reason to do that, especially to a kid?

I did three months in a youth prison for that. There

?

• Going forward as a human community, how can we prevent other groups of people from experiencing generational trauma? What places in the world today might be breeding grounds for such trauma in the future? What can we do to support those people?

were other assaults, other charges. I got put on house arrest a lot. Lots of breaching-conditions charges.

There was one woman who came into my life who was very kind to me. When I was fourteen I was dating a girl. Her mother could see I was a bad risk for bad trouble and she tried to help me by talking to me and giving me good food. She told me I could have a good future because I have a good mind and because she had seen me be kind to a lot of people. Even when her daughter and me weren't dating anymore, this woman stayed in touch with me, wanting to know how I was. I had started drinking by that point so she took me to AA [Alcoholics Anonymous] meetings and to see a counselor.

I appreciated the help but I wasn't ready. I could not get past my own plans and ideas.

I did a lot of alcohol and substantial drug use. I got drugs from people I knew. Drugs are not hard to find. I'd buy them with money I got from breaking into houses and stealing stuff and selling it. I stole cars. I know how to hotwire a car so it doesn't matter if the keys are in it or not. I was affiliated with a gang, like I said, and that's what we did.

I loved hockey. I'd been skating since I was three. Thank you, foster parents who taught me that! I played hockey from the time I was ten until I was fourteen. Another thank you to the foster parents who took me to the rink all those times! I was a good player. The coach made me an enforcer. If there was a really good player on the other team, the coach would say to me, "That guy needs to go." He'd send me in to take the good player out. I'd just fly across the ice, right into the guy, knock him down and he'd be out for the rest of the game, sometimes longer. I'd sit in the penalty box for a couple of minutes then be back on the ice.

I was playing football at school too. I got a bad head and knee injury at the same time in one game. The team doc cleared me to keep playing and the knee popped out right in the middle of the game. Both knees hurt really bad now.

I don't play sports anymore. I think I've got arthritis in at least one of my knees. I'm trying to get a knee brace for it but it costs like 500 bucks.

Jail is not too much of a difficulty for me. It's not that

Foster Care

Removing a child from their home is one of the most traumatic and disruptive steps the government can take.

Children whose families run out of money for housing are twice as likely to be placed with foster parents or in group homes ("Report Shines Light on Poverty's Role on Kids in CAS System," *Toronto Star*).

Indigenous children are 130 percent more likely to be investigated as possible victims of child abuse or neglect than white children and fifteen percent more likely to have maltreatment confirmed. They are also 168 percent more likely to be taken from their homes and placed into care ("Jailing Innocent Kids," *Toronto Star*).

Foster kids can experience nightmares, flashbacks, sudden anger and depression. They can feel they need to be on red alert all the time because they don't know what's going to happen to them next.

Foster children can be sent to many different homes and many different schools. Only 30 percent of the young people in the system are expected to graduate high school. The Canadian national average is 88 percent. Of those 30 percent who graduate, only 2 percent go on to post-secondary education. The national average of those not in care is 24 percent (www.untilthelastchild.com).

Children who grow up with their parents can still get help from their parents when they become adults — dropping in for a meal, moving back home for a while, as well as being able to continue the foundational relationship of their life.

Kids who age out of the foster-care system are just done. They are on their own, truly alone in the world. Financial support for aged-out foster youth varies, but the average nineteen-year-old leaves care with no skills, no education and no one to look after them, according to Dylan Cohen of the advocacy group First Call ("19 and Cut Off," *Globe and Mail*). According to the American Academy of Pediatrics, between 30 and 80 percent of children enter foster care with at least one physical health problem, with fully one-third entering care with a chronic health condition and up to 80 percent having significant mental-health needs.

RESOURCES FOR CHILDREN IN FOSTER CARE

The Original Foster Care Survival Guide by Paul E. Knowlton

Foster Care: A Survival Guide by Ken Marteney

A Survival Guide for Teens Aging Out of Foster Care
www.youthrightsjustice.org

What It's Like Going Into Foster Care
www.imafoster.com

much different from group homes or some of the foster homes I've been in. I've always been kind of a quiet guy, but if someone would test me I'd throw down right away so it doesn't keep happening.

I've been beat up by the cops three times. They beat me up in the cells below the court house. The stuff that goes on down there! The sense of power cops have because they have a badge and a gun. There are good cops, I know. I've met them. The ones that see you as a person and don't hit you for the fun of it. But they get a bad reputation from the bad cops.

I go to the Native Friendship Centre these days. It's a drop-in for Native people. I like doing that and I plan on going back and getting more involved there. I like being with other Native people and learning about our culture and history. It makes me feel like I have value, like I have a road to go on that's an important road. There's a lot of bias against Native people, that we use a lot of alcohol, but it was the white man who brought us alcohol in the first place.

I'd like to make it clear to you that I can't say my misfortunes were because of my surroundings. I just grew up angry and acting up.

My father's parents were abused in the residential schools. My father had a calmer life than his parents did but someone he trusted molested him and things went bad for him after that.

My mother's parents only liked kids when they were

Taking Steps ...

For yourself

Garnett finds strength in the historical cultural practices of the First Nation he belongs to. What do you find strength in? Do one thing today that helps grow your inner strength and calm.

For others

Many Indigenous communities put on traditional powwows each year that are open to the public. Find one near you and attend.

young and cute. After their kids got minds of their own, they weren't interested anymore. Mom's a real tough woman now because of that and because of what Dad did to her.

I was really looking forward to getting old enough and bold enough to confront my dad about what he did to us, how he ruined my childhood. But he died three months ago so I never got the chance. His death was hard. I went into a depression and used lots of cocaine to try to get out of it. It was hard.

I'm not using drugs now and I have a lot more control over my drinking. I've never been in treatment. I'm just trying to work on it by myself.

Right now I'm working as a laborer on building sites and on home repair sites. I'm a good worker. I enjoy making money and saving as much of it as I can.

My main dream is to go somewhere in the music industry, hip-hop in particular. I would like to become a promoter and put on shows. I've already done some of that and I really like it, getting all the details right, making sure everyone has a good time. I get a percentage from the ticket sales.

I'm a writer, too—rap music and poetry—and I like to read, especially about philosophies and conspiracies.

I see a lot of demons when I have money that I earned in the wrong way. Demons like cocaine and flashy things that bring negative attention and energy. When I have money from regular labor work, I don't see those demons.

My advice to kids in trouble? Just keep moving through it. You'll be in a different place tomorrow, and maybe it will be better.

Lamar, 18

"You have to decide not just once but over and over and over again."

Thirteen million Americans spend $60 billion a year on illegal drugs ("Do the Math: Why the Illegal Drug Business Is Thriving" by Oriana Zill and Lowell Bergman). The illegal drug business has violence and exploitation at its core, especially the exploitation of young people. From girls working in the poppy fields in Afghanistan to boys in cocaine pits in Bolivia, to kids acting as lookouts, drug runners and pushers, children around the world have their lives ruined by this industry. Somebody's getting rich. Not the children.

My mom turned me over to the police.

It was the end of the lunch period and I had a spare after that so a friend and I went downtown. We met up with someone we knew who had weed to sell. Mom happened to be driving by, saw the sale go down, pulled her car over, yanked me off the street in front of my friends, put me in her car and drove me to the police station with the pot on me.

I was charged with possession and issued a Promise to Appear notice, which meant that I promised to show up for court. I did go to court. Because of how little pot I had, I just had to go to a drug course and nothing else.

Mom and I didn't get along very well in those days. I can see now that from her point of view, turning me in was the only option for her to teach me the seriousness of what I was doing.

Would I do that to my kids? I highly doubt it, but who knows?

My mom had her first baby when she was thirteen. Her mom kicked her out for that, and she went down her own drug road, so I can't ever say she doesn't get it.

I have four sisters and five brothers. I'm the only one in conflict with the law. Dad has not been in contact with me for thirteen years and good riddance to him. He'd beat all of us. I think he's living in another city now but I don't care.

My stepfather is a long-distance truck driver. We don't always get along but he's not abusive.

How I got started in drugs was when I first started high school. I used to hang out at the smoking pit, this place just outside of school where all the smokers would go. I made friends there and they were into drugs and that's how it started.

There wasn't a drug my mom wouldn't use back when she was using and she was always afraid we would follow her on that road. When she saw me heading in that direction she did everything she could think of to straighten me out. I couldn't hear it like that though. I heard it like, "Well, you've done it so who are you to tell me not to?"

I left home and was homeless for a time. Sometimes I stayed with friends. It's one thing to crash on a friend's couch after a party. It's another thing to stay at a friend's house day after day, especially if that friend still lives with his parents and they don't really want you there! You wear out your welcome pretty fast.

So I stayed mostly on the street, sometimes under bridges. All I had were the clothes I was wearing. A lot of time I was cold. I chose the rainiest, coldest time to run away and there were many nights when I could not find a

?

• If you did not have a home to go to, where would you sleep? How would you pass the hours, especially if you had no money? How would you eat? How would you stay clean?

dry place to sleep. I'd be cold and wet all night long, and then during the day where could I go? It's a small town. There are not a lot of options when your clothes are wet and smelly and you have no money. It took all I had to survive that.

Finally I went home and asked Mom to take me back. She thought I'd learned my lesson and she let me come in. That first hot shower, those first clean clothes, that first hot meal! Until you don't have those things, you don't know how wonderful they are.

You can make a decision to stay away from drugs and do the right thing but sticking to that decision is hard. You have to decide not just once but over and over and over again. When you get involved with drugs, even in a small way like I did, you get involved with gangs. Who do you think is selling the drugs? It's gangs. I live in a small town, and there are gangs even in that town and they don't like to lose customers.

But I'm doing all right. I'm the first person in my family to graduate high school on time, with my class. I want to be a mechanic. I did a co-op placement with a truck mechanic shop, working on big engines, and they kept me on for a summer job. I hope to stay there. It's an amazing

Taking Steps ...

For yourself

Think of the adults in your life. Which of their behaviors do you not want to do in your own life? What behaviors do you admire? Write them down in two lists and think of steps you can take to move toward what you want and away from what you don't want.

For others

Pope Francis has opened a free laundromat for the homeless people of Rome. He also opened a free shower and haircutting place next to St. Peter's, and on his 78th birthday he gave away two hundred sleeping bags to people who sleep on the street. What can you do to make life easier for the kids at your school who are homeless? Is there a washer and dryer they can use? If not, can you help get laundry facilities put in?

shop with tremendous potential. We work on everything from small cars to big rigs.

To my younger self I'd have to say, "It seems like no big deal, a little drugs here and there, but all those little bits add up to bigger problems and you never know when that big thing will hit you."

Cyndy, 19

"So many things made me feel anxious."

Spending time in nature — around trees and grass and birds and wild things — is good for our health. Walking in nature can improve your memory and attention span and reduce the effects of ADHD. Being in nature also boosts cancer-fighting cells and lowers your risk of diabetes and heart attacks.

I never met my birth parents. I was a foster kid and had six foster homes. I was young for most of the changes from home to home and I didn't understand what was happening to me. I'd be in one home with one set of smells and one set of parents and one set of rules and then suddenly I'd be moved in with strangers and strange rules and strange smells. Like one house will smell of cooking and another will smell of air freshener.

This kept happening. I remember thinking even when I was little that there was something bad about me so I'd try really hard to be good but I got moved even then. Then I figured there was something deeply wrong with me, some- thing unfixable with good behavior so screw it, it wouldn't matter anyway no matter if I was good.

I have a biological sister but Children's Aid took her too,

and they put her with other people. I haven't seen her in a very long time.

My last foster home, I was in there for years. They ended up adopting me. They were okay, but they don't talk to me anymore.

When I hit middle school I started to have some mental health problems in a bad way. Lots of crying, lots of anxiety. So many things made me feel anxious. Still do, but I deal better with it now, most of the time.

Things that make me anxious? Well, the police, for one! All I have to do is *see* the police and I can feel my heart start to beat faster. It's really difficult if I have to actually talk to the police. I get afraid they're going to hurt me and make it so I can't escape.

Sometimes my anxiety made me want to do things to try to control it, like hurting myself or just staying in bed. Depression is like a thick cloud behind your eyes and in your head. You don't want to do anything. You feel bad all the time.

The other thing is that my anger was really bad. It's getting better now but I have to be really careful. Little things can make me want to explode.

Especially if people try to restrain me. I broke my adopted dad's ribs once when he was trying to restrain me.

I've had a bunch of criminal charges put on me. Some got dropped or were just warnings. The charges that stuck were obstruction of justice and assault. Here's one time. My ex-boyfriend and I were crossing the street. The cops claimed we were jaywalking. One cop asked my name and I started to have a panic attack. My boyfriend thought the cop had hit me. He hit out at his cop to try to get to me. I saw my boyfriend's cop be rough with him so I hit my cop and the other cops because by that point I was just mad and not thinking.

I've had quite a few assault charges. Theft and assault.

My adopted parents were not interested in having a daughter with mental-health problems. They took me to

?

• What makes you anxious? What happens in your body when you get anxious? What calms you? How do you feel when you are calm?

the mental ward at the hospital and left me there and that's pretty much the last I saw of them.

It didn't really surprise me. By then I was used to parents saying, "Nope, you're not for us," and getting rid of me. I was fifteen and they just left me there.

A mental hospital is like a prison and a hospital at the same time. You meet all kinds of people there, all kinds of problems. Some of the nurses are nice and try to talk to you. Some are busy and just want to give you pills, and if you don't want to take the pills they call you non-compliant and give you a shot or strap you down. It's better than jail, though. You can go into the common room and play cards or watch TV.

One good thing I will say about the police is that some of them know me now. They know about my anxiety and when they talk to me they are gentle and understanding, some of them. If I haven't done anything really bad they take me to the hospital instead of to jail.

I got expelled from school in grade ten. I've been kicked out of a few schools. Some schools refused to accept me because of my mental-health problems.

One school, I barely even attended class. I just got suspension after suspension. I got registered and went through all that but when the time came to go to class I could hardly ever do it. My social anxiety makes it hard for me to interact with other people. I don't really hang out much with others. I usually just stay by myself. If I have to do much with others, I just get scared, like I'll be hurt.

So I went into this school on this day and I got so anxious that I just couldn't do it. That made me mad because why shouldn't I be able to go to school? What's wrong with me that I can't go? Why are all these other kids better than me?

I got mad and felt like such a loser that I did something stupid. I called in a bomb threat. I didn't have a bomb—I would never do that—but I told them I did. Like, if I can't go to school, nobody can go to school. They found out it was me who did it and they kicked me out.

I had a baby that went into Children's Aid and now I'm looking forward to my second baby being born. I'm having a girl and I've already chosen a name for her, a really beautiful name because she's going to be a beautiful baby.

I'm staying in a shelter now, a shelter for homeless youth. It's good. We get food here and help with things like clothes and bus tickets and getting to appointments. It's taken its toll on my mental health though. The other kids are loud and sometimes they fight and there's lots of drama. They're all dealing with their own stuff. Most of them sleep in dormitories. I have my own room here because I'm expecting a baby, and that helps but still, it stresses me.

I don't know what I'm hoping for down the road. I'm on my own now. I was in a relationship with a guy for a couple of years but we just broke up. So I'm on my own.

School would be a good idea, since I'm going to have a baby and need to think of the future, but school is complicated because of being kicked out so many times. My anxiety might keep me out of school too.

There has to be *something* down the road. There has to be *something* good for me.

Taking Steps ...

For yourself

Take a walk in the woods. Find the natural spots in your area, big or small, and spend time with Mother Nature. Notice what happens to you.

For others

Join a tree-planting party or a clean-up crew.

Matt, 18

"Dad is dead now. I think his life was not good but at least he can't hurt anyone anymore."

When a parent goes to prison, it has a huge impact on the children left behind. If the mom goes to jail and the father is not in the picture, the children usually end up in foster care. If the dad is imprisoned, it puts the rest of the family at huge risk of becoming homeless. They lose the dad's income and there are the added costs of visits to the prison, phone calls, commissary and legal fees.

The children of prisoners have higher risks of illness, learning disorders, anxiety, behavior problems and depression. They are more likely to fall behind in school. Four percent of children in the United States have an incarcerated parent.

I grew up in foster homes. Mom lost custody of me when I was two years old. At first the Children's Aid gave me to my dad's mom, but she died. I went to my uncle's house and he was going to keep me but then the Children's Aid made me a crown ward. That means that my biological parents lost all rights to me. I didn't belong to them anymore. I belonged to the Children's Aid.

My dad wasn't able to be a dad because he was in and out of jail and prison, usually for beating up one of his girlfriends. The last time I saw him, I was at his place with him and his girlfriend. His girlfriend was joking around and gave my dad a little slap on the butt.

Dad flipped out. He went wild. He started punching her and then he picked up a baseball bat and attacked her with the bat.

I ran out of there and yelled for the police. I wanted to stay and help my dad's girlfriend because I really liked her and she was always nice to me, but I'd seen my dad like that before. If I tried to come between them we would have both been killed, and I was too small to bring him down. So I did the best thing I could think of.

The cops came and dragged him off her and away. The ambulance took the girlfriend. She was in a coma for months.

Dad is dead now. I think his life was not good but at least he can't hurt anyone anymore.

I've got thirteen high-school credits. Thirteen and a half, actually. Everyone who knows me will tell you that I love school and I really do. I love being around all the school stuff. Sometimes I like being around the teachers too, if they seem to not mind when I don't always understand something right away. Some teachers will stick with you until you get it, even if they have to explain it five times because they can tell you're paying attention. Others do it once and if you don't get it, that's not their problem.

Other kids can be discouraging. Some are okay but you can never be sure. They can seem okay one minute then they are out to get you.

School work is hard for me, especially math. I can do addition and subtraction okay, but things like long division and fractions get jumbled up. I get mad then and refuse to do it.

I was always a troubled kid. I guess I was a mean kid. I got to look at my Children's Aid reports and there's all these reports where they write that I pushed kids, tripped kids. One day in grade six I picked up a chair and just started swinging. I destroyed the whole classroom. I don't

remember why or what I was angry at. I do remember that
the police came and they evacuated the whole school. It
was almost the end of the day though, so everyone got to
go home early.

I had this one friend, I'll call him Randy. Before my
dad died we were best friends. After Dad died we grew
apart because I didn't want to be around anyone. One day
this Randy made a comment to me about Dad and I beat
him up.

I started getting in trouble with the law when I was
eleven. I was charged when I was twelve with stealing a
car. I went to a John Howard twelve-week program for
that. It was okay. They talked to me about the charges and
about changing my life.

I kept on doing what I was doing. They kicked me out
of so many schools and agencies and foster homes. Nobody
wanted me around. I'd steal from grocery stores. I broke
into cars.

I never had a fear of anything. I kept weapons on me,
knives and extenders, mostly. Extenders are like clubs
that extend when you swing them. I knew I could defend
myself from whatever. I never had too much to do with
guns. I only had two or three guns in my whole life.

One of my foster moms was really great. I still talk to
her, and every time we say goodbye she says, "I love you." I
helped her with the younger kids when I lived with her.

What happened there was that I just got out of jail and

was messed up. I went into her foster home to live and there was this kid there who kept yelling at me. He'd yell stupid stuff and would not leave me alone. So I punched him to shut him up. That meant I couldn't stay in that foster home anymore, but that foster mom hugged me and said she knew I was good and that she loved me.

Jail. Lots of jail for me. I went to open custody when I was twelve. Open custody is like a regular house. You share a room with other kids, you wear your own clothes, you can walk out the front door. They don't lock you in. You eat regular food. You've got a lot of people in your business, but it's not bad.

One of the secure facilities I was in was also not bad because they had real food to eat. You could see it being made in the kitchen and it was good, so you knew that no matter how bad the day went, you'd have a meal that was okay.

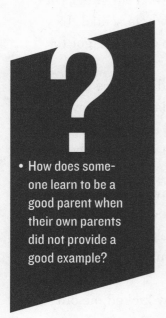

• How does someone learn to be a good parent when their own parents did not provide a good example?

The youth prison—that's a real penitentiary! I've been there a lot. The food there is not good. It comes out of boxes and I think a lot of it they got cheap because it's expired. I cut into a fish cake once and there was green on the inside. They replay the same meals over and over again three times a week. We even formed a little committee to talk to the superintendent about it to see if he would change the meals. He wouldn't, but I never saw him eat that food!

The youth pen gives you levels that you can work on to earn privileges.

The Bronze level, you go to bed at nine o'clock. Silver, you get 9:30 bedtime. Gold, you go to bed at 10 p.m. and can have a portable DVD player in your room for two hours once a week. Platinum is the highest level. You get a 10:30 bedtime, you can sometimes watch TV or play video games and you get the Saturday incentive meal, like from KFC or Domino's Pizza.

I got three high-school credits while I was in the youth pen, so in that way it was useful.

The COs—Corrections Officers, you don't dare call them guards—some are good, some are not. The new ones are all stuck to the rules and they're trying to show they're not afraid of us. The ones that have been around for a bit, well, some of them are jerks but others can relax and look at us like we are people and not just things to be locked up.

Everyone knows me there because I've been there so much. They have a nickname for me, a friendly one. They treat me with respect so I treat them with respect right back. I only ran at two staff there.

I started selling drugs when I was sixteen. A friend got me into it. That led to more charges.

I have twenty-three convictions as a youth. Now I'm eighteen and an adult. If you get an adult charge your youth charges can be brought over into your new record, so

Seeing the Blows

When children witness violence between their parents, they start to believe that it is normal to hit and be hit in relationships. Girls who grow up in violence often end up with men who beat them the way their father beat their mother. Boys who grow up seeing their mothers abused often grow up to treat women in their lives just as badly — they have had no role models to teach them differently.

CASA for Children says, "Children not only watch the abuse. They hear the sounds of abuse, see the bruises and, of course, they, too, are the victims. They are taught to keep the family secret. They suffer in silence and shame."

When babies and small children are around violence, they can become irritable, afraid to be separated from their moms, have trouble sleeping and trouble toilet training. Older children can suffer from depression, find it hard to concentrate in school and have anxiety that can lead to problems like bedwetting.

Children in this situation can heal once the violence is removed, if they are given support to understand what they have been through and to learn ways to solve problems without violence.

If you live in a home where there is violence, know that it is never about you. The adults may blame you, but that is just their own inside mess talking. If you did not exist, they would still behave this way. You did not cause it. You cannot fix it. Your job is to protect yourself and get help to grow into the sort of human being you want to be.

(With thanks to "Domestic Violence Has Long Range Consequences," www.casaforchildren.wordpress. com, and "Little Eyes, Little Ears: How Violence Against a Mother Shapes Children as They Grow," by Alison Cunningham and Linda Baker.)

they don't disappear like you might think. There's no such thing as a clean slate when you turn eighteen.

I was just breached on probation, so now I have an adult record. The breaches, they get you with the breaches. They put these rules on you and if you break them it's a crime. I kept telling Children's Aid to give me my freedom and they wouldn't do it. They told me to do this job they lined up for me and one day I didn't want to go to work and that was a breach of conditions, a criminal charge. One day I wanted to go see my girlfriend and they said, "If you walk outside you'll get breached." You can never get out of it.

I've got to figure this out because I'm having a baby next month, a baby girl. The baby's mom is out in another province and she wants full custody. Okay with that, but I want to still be a dad somehow, a better dad than my dad was. So I've got to get this figured out.

Taking Steps ...

For yourself

Matt talks about the joy of eating real food in some of the places he was sent to, instead of the institutional food from packages. Cook yourself and your family and friends a meal of real food.

For others

Say something kind to a person you don't usually talk to. You never know the sort of day they are having.

Zach, 18

"Some pills will just kill your liver. Other pills will kill parts of your brain and leave you like a vegetable."

Homeless youth are at greater risk of dying from suicide. Feeling powerless feeds suicidal thoughts. When we feel we can control things in our lives, it helps us believe we have other choices.

I got stabbed in the street when I was fifteen. It was over a girl. The guy who stabbed me was twenty-one. He was a really big guy. I was really small compared to him. He stabbed me in the back.

He claimed in court that he had schizophrenia and that we were both drinking and that he wanted that girl to be dating him only she didn't want to and I got in his way.

I was living on the streets at that point. He came up behind me and stabbed me in the back. I didn't know what happened until I woke up in the children's hospital. At least I got to sleep in a bed that night.

My parents split up when I was eight. They had a big custody battle. I lived with Mom because Dad drank and did cocaine, but he doesn't do that now.

I lived with Mom from the time I was eight until I was fifteen. Seven years. She was really strict and she beat me

?

• Zach's foster mom taught him how to eat at a table with other people during meal times. Why do you think that was such a big deal to him?

when I didn't follow all of her rules. I mean, she beat me so hard I had blood blisters all over me, all kinds of bruises.

Here's one time when she beat me. I had a paper route and I didn't want to do it anymore. I had ninety-eight customers, more than any of the other carriers, but I was paid the same as them for doing a lot more work. So I wanted to quit. She beat me for that.

She drank and worked at a bar. She drank at work and came home drunk in the middle of the night. She'd wake me up and beat me. She'd beat me in the afternoon too, in front of my friends.

One night she beat me so bad I just left. I ran away with just what I was wearing, nothing else. I just wanted to not get hit anymore. I didn't care about more than that.

I lived the whole summer after grade eight on the streets of this small city. I don't know if Mom even went out looking for me or if she reported me missing or even noticed I was gone.

Where did I sleep? I slept under bridges, in parks, in doorways, sometimes on someone's lawn furniture in their backyard, or I'd find a shed that wasn't locked. I often roamed around at night picking up bottles to sell to have money to eat.

In a way it was good. I was free and I wasn't being hit or around Mom's drinking. It was also hard. I was hungry and always on edge and always wondering where to sleep. If I go to this place will I be rolled? If I go to this other place will the cops find me? Am I going to get rained on or bit up by mosquitoes? Mosquitoes really get you in the morning.

So I was on the streets until I got stabbed. He stabbed me three times in the back and the shoulder. And I went to the hospital.

I went to foster homes after that.

I tried to kill myself last July. They say if you take enough Tylenol it will be your last headache. But it's not that simple. It's hard to die from pills. You could throw them up before they do any good. Some pills will just kill your liver. Other pills will kill parts of your brain and leave you like a vegetable.

I'm glad I didn't die. I think I've got stuff to do.

I'd like to travel. I've never left this province. I'd like to see the rest of the country and maybe even go to Cuba. You can go to Cuba for, like $700. I'd like to get into the trades, maybe be a master carpenter, if I can learn how to do the work. I used to keep a journal before I got stabbed. The knife messed up my shoulder muscle and arm so I don't write as much now.

If my parents didn't drink, my life would have been better, or if they drank less or if they didn't get violent. All that would have made my life better.

I started drinking. Why wouldn't I? But now I've stopped. I signed up for a youth Alcoholics Anonymous. They say don't drink and don't smoke but instead do healthy things and have healthy goals, so that's what I'm trying to do.

I did have one great foster mom. She really threw me a lifeline. She taught me manners, like how to hold the door for someone, how to eat at a table with other people at meal times, how to clean my room and keep it clean. She said there's no reason why I can't do these things and do all the other things that people do, like have a job or a bank account.

Taking Steps ...

For yourself

Think of all the places in your life where you feel you have no power. Examine one of these places and find one thing you can do to make you feel you have more power and choice in that situation. For example, if you hate school and feel forced into going, what changes can you make that give you more control over what that experience is like?

For others

Where can people go for help in your community when they are thinking of giving it all up? Could you put up one of their posters at your supermarket, library, school or some other place in your neighborhood?

You just have to power through it. Don't settle into your sadness and your life will get easier. Last year I was stressing about something that's passed now. Next year there will be something else, some new problems. Don't get too bugged about what's going on now because it will change. Time will change it.

Someday I'd like to have a kid. There's a quote I heard that I like, that I would try to live by if I ever have a kid. "Don't give me what you couldn't have, teach me what you wish you'd been taught."

That's what I'd like to give my kid.

Lindy, 19

"I saw too many things a child should not have to see."

When a child lives with a parent who is mentally ill, their lives can be marred by chaos and neglect. Although it is completely possible for someone who is mentally ill to be a good parent, the illness can also be overwhelming.

If the parent goes in and out of treatment, children deal with repeated separations. The child will find ways to take the blame for the parent's pain, and the parent will sometimes blame the child. Often the oldest child will assume the responsibilities of mom or dad, looking after the home and their younger siblings and the ill parent. They may be embarrassed by their parent's illness, or even ashamed, especially if other kids find out about it and use it against them. So, in addition to everything else, they have the burden of keeping a secret ("Growing Up with a Mentally Ill Parent: 6 Core Experiences" by Vinita Mehta, *Psychology Today*).

For the first eight years of my life I lived in a big city. Then I moved to a small town. It was a hard town to move to when I was already feeling weird. Plus I had attended a French immersion school in the city. I could read and write in French but not at all in English, so I went from being near the top of my class to being near the bottom.

The first eight years of my life were not pretty. It was not all puppies and rainbows. There was a lot of abuse. I saw too many things a child should not have to see. I spent most of those years being very afraid.

My parents split. The court made the wrong decision. They said I should go with Mom even though all the evidence showed she was unfit to look after kids. Mom moved me and my little sister to this small town and then things went really, really bad.

My little sister was born when I was five. I promised myself that nothing bad would happen to her, that I would protect her. I knew that meant I would have to take most of the beatings. But I would have felt worse if I had to watch my little sister get hit.

My mother was mentally ill and would not take her pills. She was just a mess, moody and frantic and all over the place.

My dad basically ran out on us and my sister's dad also ran out on us. My dad is more like a bachelor uncle than a dad. I can't take him seriously because he did not protect us.

My real parents—the ones I consider the real parents, the ones who raised me — were Mom's parents, my grandparents. Both of them are dead now. Grandma died in a fire, a particularly awful way to die.

Mom would not feed us or care for us. My sister was only three. She couldn't understand what was going on, but I was eight. I could see that we had very little food in the house. I could not ask Mom to get more for us. She was already raging and you couldn't ask her for anything. I took the food we had and I rationed it to make it last for the rest of the month. I gave most of it to my sister. I didn't go to school that whole month because I was afraid Mom would hurt my sister.

After a month or so of this there was no help coming from anybody. I packed two bags, one for me and one for my sister. The night before I left I prayed to whoever was listening that my sister or me wouldn't get hurt on our escape.

I was very weak from not eating. I only had my bike

to use to escape with. I couldn't take my sister on my bike and that was all I had! I couldn't walk either. If I was going to get away it had to be fast in case Mom came running out after me.

Mom fell asleep in the afternoon and that's when I escaped.

I pedaled like mad to Grampa's house and I told them what was going on. They hadn't seen Mom in a long while because she wouldn't let them. When I showed up at their house they were very worried. Grampa and I went back to our apartment building. I went with him because I wasn't sure my sister would remember him and she would need to see me when he brought her out. I told him where our bags were, where my sister was and he went in to rescue her.

I never believed in knights in shining armor until that day.

Grampa had to break down the door to get into the apartment, which woke Mom up. He had to really fight to get my sister out, but he did. He saved my sister.

We never bathed when we were with Mom. We never had clean clothes or clean hair. The first thing that happened when we got to Grampa and Grandma's house is that we had a bath. Grandma cried when she helped me out of the bathtub. I was so malnourished! I saw myself in the bathroom mirror and I looked like a skeleton with my eyes all sunk in.

Grandma put me in jammies and she put me to bed. Then she called the police.

The police arrived and they came into the bedroom to talk to me. When they mentioned my mother, I hid under the bed. Many cops had to drag me out. They tried to get me to go back to Mom and I just went back under the bed.

They let me and my sister stay with Grandma and Grampa.

I was like a zombie for weeks. I went around with a blank face. I didn't know what to do or how to be. I wasn't used to living in a safe, clean, calm place. I didn't know how not to be afraid all the time. Grandma said I looked like a lost soul.

Then they got me a dog, a happy little dog named Chloe, and that made things better. I started to relax around Chloe.

I was okay for a bit but then came the flashbacks and the PTSD. Soldiers aren't the only ones to get PTSD. Beaten-up children get it too. I battled with that all through school.

I couldn't stay forever with my grandparents because they were not well and they had no room for my sister and me long-term. We were put into foster care.

Foster care was when I started to have regular contact with the police. I kept running away from foster homes and the police kept picking me up and bringing me back to the police station where I'd sit and wait to be taken to another foster home. Foster homes made me not feel safe again because there was chaos with some of the families. I started having flashbacks and a short temper. I was attacking people so that they wouldn't attack me.

I was hungry and filthy and an all-round mess. Some of my teachers tried to help. At least one of them called Mom on the phone but Mom was a good actress. She put on a fake voice and told them some lie, like, "My daughter just has mono" or "She's got the flu again." So some of the teachers tried.

The PTSD got so bad that I had to take a year off high

?

• Lindy talks about never being clean when she lived with her mom. How might that make a child feel? What could be done at your school so that a child in that situation can get herself clean and get clean clothes before they go to class?

school. I couldn't sit in a classroom without shaking. I couldn't be around a lot of people who made loud noises. I couldn't be in the crowds moving through the halls. I kept having panic attacks.

I eventually got help. I got on the right meds and learned how soldiers cope with PTSD, like meditation and deep breathing. I carry lavender buds around with me because the scent is so relaxing.

I never got charged when I lashed out at people, even though I rode in the back of many, many police cars. I guess they knew my history and they gave me a break. That is one good thing about a small town. The police are able to get to know you and they know your story and if they are compassionate, they watch out for you in a good way. They watched out for me, anyway.

Well, some did. Not all. I've had cops wake me up with their steel-toed boots on my head or in my ribs when I've been sleeping in a park.

I am so glad I never got charged. I've met kids in the system who were charged and I am so grateful I never had to go through that.

I finished high school and I went to college for film and television production. I love facts, especially facts about history, all periods of history. I like looking at how the past created the present.

I think I have a chance to make it.

Taking Steps ...

For yourself

Do you take on other people's problems as your own? Who and what do you worry about? If there is something you can do about a problem, try to do it. If there isn't, can you let it go? You don't need to carry the whole world. Others can shoulder some of the burden.

For others

Talk to your teacher and see if they will incorporate two minutes of quiet, deep breathing into every class to give everyone a mental timeout and a moment to relax.

Not all wars have been overseas with guns. Some wars are in the home and with people who should care about you. I don't know if I'll ever get rid of the pain I'm carrying. Maybe I can turn it into something not so heavy.

Benny, 15

"I started hanging around with the wrong people. It was something to do."

To be bored is to feel trapped. It is the feeling of being stuck somewhere we don't want to be with no way to entertain ourselves. For both old and young, many unwise decisions have been made in an effort to escape boredom.

Sports facilities, theater groups, music lessons, art studios and other places where kids can go to explore their interests and build their skills are good investments for any community.

I was born in a city in the middle of the country, then moved out east to live with my dad. He's from the east. Mom's from here. Mom lived with us for a bit when we were out east but she and Dad were fighting all the time so she came back here.

She has a new boyfriend now. He's a roofer.

Dad has a new girlfriend too. He's a lobster fisherman. I helped him when I was out there. I went out on the boat, lifting lobster traps, taking out the lobsters. We were right out on the ocean in this little boat and I loved it. It's hard work. You work so hard your body hurts, and the ocean can turn on you. When it's storming it's scary. The waves get high and I was afraid but probably because I wasn't used to it.

That part of being out east was good, and I like the look of the place too, the hills and the winding roads and the trees and the ocean. It's not all flat and boring like it is around here. I also started getting into trouble out there. I started hanging around with the wrong people. It was something to do.

The first time I broke the law, me and two friends were out looking at cars, just going from one to another on the street—yes, we like this one, no, this one's a piece of crap. That kind of thing. Then we saw that one of the cars still had the keys in it.

We didn't even think about it. We just looked at each other, got in the car and went for a ride. When we were done, we left the car somewhere, unharmed, keys inside, and that was that.

It was so easy and so fun. It became like a game, looking for cars with keys and going for rides. We just kept doing it. My heart would race and I'd get this energy and it felt really good.

We learned how to steal cars even without the keys. It was so easy to steal, we just kept doing it. Some nights we'd steal more than one. Steal the first one, drive it somewhere, leave it, steal another. We weren't going anywhere in particular. We were just, like, going.

Here's how we got caught.

I guess the police were on to us or maybe we were speeding. They started chasing us. We had stolen this truck. There were a bunch of us in the truck, me and my friends, a couple of other kids, some girls we'd picked up. I had a girl sitting on my lap. The police were chasing us and we were driving fast to try to get away. My friend was driving. He wasn't very good at it because we crashed into a couple of parked cars.

When the truck crashed to a stop we all got out and started running in all directions. Well, I did, anyway. I just took off. I don't think anyone was hurt. Maybe we were too drunk to get hurt, if that makes any sense.

The police were busy arresting the driver and the other kids who were too dazed or scared or drunk to run away, and I was able to get away.

The police found me after, though. I didn't know where we'd got to. I wasn't paying attention to that. I was in a city I didn't know. I was drunk and maybe shell-shocked and acting really stupid. Some guy in the neighborhood filmed me and called the police.

They arrested me and called my parents, who were not happy!

I was charged with joy riding, mischief, taking a car without the owner's consent, breaching probation, fleeing from the police—was that all? Maybe public intoxication too. A bunch of charges. I got out on a Promise to Appear. I went to court and a legal-aid lawyer represented me.

I got sentenced to two weeks in a youth facility. It wasn't too bad because I could wear my own clothes and a friend was in there with me.

Well, that wasn't the end of it. I kept on getting into trouble and got shipped back here to this province because my parents thought that might straighten me out.

I've been arrested back here a few times. Mostly for fighting. Me and my girl were fighting one time and I got charged with assault and I got charged for assaulting Mom's boyfriend and for more drinking things.

When you're first arrested you get put in a holding cell. It's just a bare cold room with concrete benches to sleep on and a toilet that's right in the open for everyone to see. You're given these crappy sandwiches to eat and some kind of foul fruit stuff to drink.

You have nothing to do. No TV, no books. You just sit or sleep or talk to other kids. Or you fight or you try to avoid a fight. It's nasty.

Then you go to bail court. If someone bails you out, that's good. You get to leave after you sign all the crazy conditions they come up with that you have to agree to if you want to get out, like not being out of the house after six o'clock at night. You agree to them in order to leave but nobody believes you'll keep your promise. It just gives them something else to charge you with—breaching conditions—when they pick you up the next time.

If you don't make bail you get sent to a reformatory. At least I did.

The youth facility here is not like the one out east. Here it's basically a penitentiary for kids. You have to wear a uniform—dark red track pants, dark red T-shirt, dark red sweater. Nobody feels dressed up in that. You just feel sloppy.

When you get to the facility you have to get strip-searched, which is just as bad in real life as it looks like in the movies. Then you shower and put on your prison clothes. Then you go sit down with a staff and they take down all your information.

You get your own room. It has a door with a window in it. It has a metal bed with a really thin piece of padding on it. Not comfortable at all. You get one blanket. No pillow.

Bedtime is 9:30 and you're locked in your cell until 7:30 in the morning. You get up to do chores like cleaning the bathroom, sweeping the floor, cleaning the common room. There's a school in the building and you march there as a group. You say, "Yes, miss," to the teachers and "Yes, sir."

I have to say, though, that the staff, maybe most of them, are nice and even funny, at least they have been with me. There are some kids there, though, well, let me just say it's not all fun and games.

For punishments they put you in OP—that's Off Privileges. You're locked in your cell for twenty-four hours and your food is brought to you. They let you out to go to the toilet and that's it.

If you get in big trouble they take you to a whole different unit. You are totally locked down there in solitary. There's even a toilet in your cell. I haven't had to do that, but the other kids told me about it.

I'm out of jail now but I don't know for how long. I've got charges pending again. Assault charges and two breaches.

• What do you do when you feel bored?
• What makes others in your family feel bored? How do they deal with it?

The crown wants me to do some serious time this time but I hope I don't.

I used to play soccer. I really enjoyed it and want to be a soccer player again. I don't smoke cigarettes so I can run for a long time. The booze and weed are probably not good for me, soccer-wise, but I could stop doing them and really get into serious shape.

The other thing I really like is science. In my science course right now I'm studying cellular respiration and eco systems, about the way cells use energy. It's about everything being connected and one little thing affecting even big things.

I never thought about the people whose cars I took. I thought about the car, not the owner. A chaplain at a reformatory asked me to think about the people and imagine what it would be like for them to have their car stolen. Maybe one of the cars was owned by a mom with a baby and a lot of bags of groceries coming back to her car and it was gone, or maybe it was owned by a person who couldn't walk very far or who was taking a family member with cancer to the doctor. I had just made all those people have a worse day.

Taking Steps ...

For yourself

Break out of your routine! Do something different today — even something small that will help you see yourself and your world in a new way. Go home from school by a different route. Sit beside a different kid on the bus. Have a conversation with someone you usually ignore. Go to the library and look through a book you would normally never pick up. Do some research on local things you could do to add some zip to your life.

For others

In the TV show M*A*S*H, during long periods of boredom during the Korean War, the doctors at the army field hospital organized a company sock wash — doing an ordinary, dull task but with others and in a party-like way. What dull, ordinary thing could you and your friends turn into your own version of a sock wash?

The point is, you don't know whose car you're taking. You could be stealing the car of some jerk who just beat up his wife and messed with his kid, who deserves to have bad things happen to him. But if you take his car, he's going to go back into that house and beat up his wife again, and that's going to be on you. I never thought about all that before.

Maybe thinking about that will help me stop. I hope so. I can do jail and court and all that. But maybe there's something better out there for me to do.

A Brother's Story

Both of my older brothers were criminally active as kids, in and out of custody. I watched my parents deal with them and go through it—their worry, their stress, their hope that this time would be the last time and then going back into it again when my brothers committed another crime.

My parents were born in the late 1950s. In the seventies and eighties, they had a hippie mentality, lots of drug use, going to rock shows, not being too concerned about things like bills and planning for the future. A few years before they were married they were both in a bad motorcycle accident. My father lost his legs. Mom had terrible internal injuries. They both took a lot of pain meds which they became addicted to—pain meds and alcohol. By the time I was seven or eight years old, they were both going in and out of drug and alcohol rehab.

When they were not in rehab they were working. Mom worked in a grocery store for twenty-three years and she did factory work. She always seemed to be working two or three jobs at one time. Dad too. We had a lot of babysitters.

At one point in her life, Mom was doing cocaine. Until she had grandchildren she drank and used drugs almost every weekend. Now she's quit smoking and her and Dad don't drink anymore. They use some drugs but only for pain management. Dad was put on a fentanyl patch a few years ago. Fentanyl is one hundred times stronger than heroin. I watched him detox off of that, so I certainly don't look down on him for just using marijuana now.

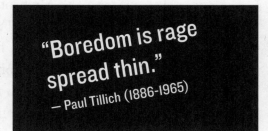

"Boredom is rage spread thin."
— Paul Tillich (1886-1965)

As a boy I was not embarrassed by them being in rehab. I think it was commendable for them to be facing their problems head on.

My older brothers did a lot of break and enters, breaking into places and stealing things to sell for drugs or for kicks. We grew up in a small city. My brothers got a reputation with the police. I had an upstairs bedroom overlooking the street and I don't know how many times I looked out the window to see the police bringing one or both brothers home after catching them doing something. They were picked up so many times and given warnings before they were finally charged.

One time the cops banged on our door to get my brothers and arrest them. I remember my mother crying and begging the police not to use the handcuffs.

It didn't really surprise me to see them arrested. I knew they were thieves because they were always stealing from our parents and our parents were sometimes too out of it to notice.

Both brothers were found guilty that time. The oldest one had to go into youth detention in another city for some months. I forget how many. He never got arrested again after that but only because he never got caught. He kept on with criminal activity until he had children of his own, then he stopped. Up until then though, he was active in theft and in selling drugs. I knew this because his buddies would come up to me and hand me the money they owed him.

My other brother got sent to an outdoor survival-skill program in a provincial park. It was sort of a boot camp detention center. A lot of the boys hated it, he said, but it worked for him. He came home totally changed into a new way of thinking, and he's been doing good things ever since.

My brothers were quite a bit older than me and mostly protected me from their criminal activity. Not that I was an angel, but I was never arrested or in trouble with the law for something I did. I think I just got lucky. I was always in fights. I know I hurt people, trying to make a name for myself. I looked on it as defending my friends, but it really was more sinister than that.

I was never arrested but I did have to spend time with the police when I was really young, like in first grade.

There was a serious bully-type incident in the bathroom at my school. I was the last person in the bathroom before the incident. The police interrogated me because one of the bullies tried to put the blame on one of my brothers. Almost no one really believed that my brother didn't do it because he had a bad reputation.

The interrogation laws back then were different from what they are today. The police separated me from my parents. They put me in a small room with a two-way mirror, a small table and two cops. They asked me questions over and over. They asked me questions that a six-year-old could not possibly understand.

I felt like *I* was in trouble.

The interrogation practices have changed since then. Now parents can be in the room when their child is questioned.

At the trial it all came down to my testimony that I did not see my brother in the bathroom and there was also a teacher who testified that my brother was with her.

I went to court when I was an older child but only as a spectator, when my brothers were on trial. I felt that I was mostly there to support my parents. They were not really surprised by what my brothers did. They felt a lot of guilt because of the way their drinking and drug abuse created chaos in our daily lives—the drinking especially and the fights that came from the drinking.

I was so lucky not to get caught when I was younger because when you get caught you get put into the system, and it's really hard to get out of it. Because I was never in the system I was more easily able to get out of the lifestyle. I had an exit. I had no criminal record, no one I had to report to. I could leave it behind and go to school. I worked hard, did well and graduated with honors.

Now I work with kids in crisis, kids doing the same stuff I did only without parents pulling for them. When kids get into the system they end up believing the labels they are given. It takes a lot of work to change those beliefs.

Iris, 16

"I remember hoping that the cuffs were locked so tight he could not get out of them."

A 2016 youth homelessness survey estimates that nearly one-third of homeless young are lesbian, gay, bisexual or transgendered (www. homelesshub.ca). Even though we have come a long way as a society in terms of accepting one another for who we are, we still have a long way to go. Too many kids are kicked out when they come out. Life on the street subjects them to violence in all forms and puts them in danger of death from diseases or from crime.

I'm one of those proud gay girls. If you don't like gay, I'll try to make you like *me,* and then you'll have no reason to be against gays. I try to be positive and to spread that around.

I've been involved with Children's Aid since I was seven and a half months old. I'm staying in a shelter now. Some Children's Aid workers are all surface, just get the day done and go home. Others really seem to want to help kids.

My birth father went to jail when I was a baby. After he was arrested, my mother took off with me and my older brothers. My brothers told me that we left a house with everything—food, clothes, everything, but Mom just took us and left.

She had a new boyfriend and she was into partying. The boyfriend was a bad guy, especially when the drugs ran out. He didn't like us kids and Mom didn't care that he didn't as long as the drugs kept coming. One night they were both stoned and hitting us. My older brother ran out and got the police. They came and arrested my stepfather. I remember the police pulling my stepfather's hands behind his back and putting the handcuffs on him. I remember hoping that the cuffs were locked so tight he could not get out of them.

I hardly ever went to school when I was little. Mom didn't take me. We moved around a lot and she wouldn't bother to re-register me in the new place so I just stayed home. For months and months I'd be at home.

I was in fourth grade and in foster care before I had to go to school regularly. It was hard. I didn't know what to do. I didn't know how to behave in a school or a classroom. I didn't know how to talk to anyone. I didn't know how to act with the other kids and they would laugh at me. That would make me mad, so I'd get in trouble. That's how it went for me for a long time.

My first time being charged was when I was arrested for smoking pot on school property just before my birthday. Then I was charged for assaulting my ex-girlfriend.

I got a mischief charge for breaking my bedroom door in the foster home. I was mad and hit the door instead of hitting the person, and the door broke. The foster mom wasn't bothered about it at the time. She said, "Better to hit a door than to hit someone." But two days later she was mad at me for talking back to her and she called the police. I was out walking to the bus stop and the police car pulled up beside me. The cops got out, cuffed me and put me in the back of the cop car. They said I was being arrested for destruction of property.

I asked them, "Why are you doing this now? I broke the door two days ago and the foster mom said it was no big deal?"

The cop said, "I guess she changed her mind."

They drove me back to the foster home and one of the other kids there confirmed my story. The police weren't too excited about it then. They figured my foster mom was just in a bad mood, but they still charged me with mischief because I had damaged someone else's property. I didn't have to go to jail for that. I got to do a diversion program instead, community service hours.

I didn't want to stay in that foster home so I headed over to my aunt's house and stayed there for a bit. I got in more trouble with a door—this time at school. I damaged a door there. I was charged with mischief under $5000 again. I was taken into custody for that and let go with conditions on where I was supposed to live until the trial. Sometimes you'll be arrested and just given conditions right at the station. You don't always have to go to court. Depends on the charges.

They said I had to stay with my aunt but I had a fight with her. I went to stay somewhere else for a few days. When I got back to my aunt's house I got arrested for breaching conditions.

That time they took me into custody. I had to spend sixteen hours in a cell in the central police station. It was the worst. Don't ever go there if you can help it. I was very scared. It was freezing in there and all I had on were shorts and a tank top.

You walk in and face a counter. You have to place your hands on this X in just the right way or the police will put them there for you. You have to look straight ahead while they search you. One cop asked me a question during the search and I turned my head to answer her, out of respect, because it's polite to look at someone who's talking to you. They came right down on me for that! All you can do is what they tell you to do.

They take everything off you that you could possibly use to hurt yourself or that someone could steal. They take your fingerprints and photographs. Then they put you in a cell and you sit there, shivering, scared and hungry.

They gave me a pack of sandwiches at some point.

Awful sandwiches. I didn't eat them. I used them as a pillow. At night they gave me a smelly blanket with holes in it. The bed was metal, no mattress. I hate being locked in anywhere and it was a small cell.

I went to court over a video camera and TV screen. I was released on my own undertaking. I didn't have to post bail. I just had to promise to show up for trial.

I go to court for that this Friday. If I miss that court date I'll get more charges. My conditions include that I can't carry lighters or perfume or anything that can be used as explosives.

I'm hoping that my aunt will be in court with me so I won't be alone, but I'm also hoping she won't be there because I don't want her to see me like that. She already doesn't really like me.

I left her house because she wouldn't let me date my girlfriend. She doesn't like me being gay.

I got raped by two men in the city a little bit ago. I called the police and did a rape kit, all the things you're supposed to do when you get raped. One of the rapists is in custody now. The other is still on the run.

There are people on the street who know the men raped me. These people told me that if I complete my statement about it and these guys go away for it, I'll get beat up worse than I could ever dream would happen.

I'm still going to finish my statement though. Some people don't belong in jail. Those rapists belong behind bars!

I went back to my aunt's house after doing the rape kit, hoping she would let me stay, but she asked if I still liked girls. When I said yes, she threw me out again. So I went to a shelter, and they gave me a bed.

At the end of the day, most of my problems will go away. I try to be happy when people are sad because maybe I can make them happy too. As soon as I walk into the shelter I say, "Hey, hey, hey!" and that good energy perks people up.

Mom's disowned me again. She does that a lot. Once she refused to talk to me for four years.

• With all that has happened to her, how do you think Iris manages to try to be happy? Do you think kids in foster care are treated differently than kids who live with their own families? Why is this?

But that's her.

This is me.

I'm doing good. I try to cut out all the drama in my life. I'm trying to save up enough money so my girlfriend and I can go to the Dominican so we can have a nice holiday in a beautiful place.

I have great energy. I try to be happy and open to everyone and I try not to let what happened before drag me down again.

I know who I am.

Taking Steps ...

For yourself

When things seem to be falling apart around you, it can help to have something you enjoy that is constant, like art, sports, science, music, collecting buttons — anything! What do you have that is a constant source of joy for you? If you don't have something now, spend some time thinking of what you might like.

For others

Decide to send out only cheerful, positive energy into the world today, even if you have woken up in a bad mood. Do kind things for people, smile at strangers on the street, thank your parents and teachers, help out someone younger and less popular. Take note of how people respond and how you feel at the end of the day.

Jake, 18

"If I had hung around kids who liked to do things instead of just prove how tough they were, then I would have done interesting, positive things too."

We don't have to live in anger. Even if terrible things have been done to us, we can learn to respect ourselves, our strengths and have admiration for our ability to push through hard times. Just because someone abused us, we don't have to believe we deserved it. We can learn to separate our story from our abuser's. Anger management classes can sometimes help with that by teaching us about our emotions and the choices we have.

I was involved with the justice system for three years when I was younger. I got in a lot of fights. Kids would talk crap to me at school and that would make me fight them.

I attended seven different schools. My parents separated when I was six. I was raised by Dad. He works for a cleaning company. Mom moved nine hours away with my two brothers and my sister. One of my brothers is also in trouble for fighting.

For me the fighting started really early. I always hated having to deal with kids who thought they were tough. They'd bug me, try to poke me into fighting.

In grade one I got suspended for breaking a kid's glasses. This kid was in a Coke commercial and he wouldn't shut up bragging about it.

?

- What could have been done for Jake when he was still very young to help him deal with his anger and channel his energies into something that could work for him? Do you remember being really mad when you were small? What calmed you? What makes you mad now? How do you deal with it?

By grade two I was expelled. I was always an angry kid. I always felt that I needed to be tough.

So I went to a different school and I punched a teacher. He threw a stick at me first. We were playing soccer. It must have been gym class. The teacher was on the other team and I scored on him. He threw a stick at me so I punched him. He was fired. I was expelled again.

I went to another school to go to grade seven, then I was expelled again. I was a new kid and all the other kids tried to challenge me. That made me angry and that's why I was expelled.

In all this time, even with all these fights, I loved playing basketball. As long as I could play basketball and the kids didn't challenge me and the teachers didn't slam me, I was fine. I was good.

At the beginning of grade eight I had to meet with the school board and promise to behave. I spent grade eight in a school where I didn't know anybody. Nobody had any preconceived notions about who I was, so no one pushed at me. They just let me play basketball. The year went by without any problems.

In high school there were more fights and I got kicked out again. I saw a kid slap his girlfriend and I flattened him. The kid's family pressed charges against me. The school kicked me out. I was charged two more times for assaulting the same kid. He kept goading me on and I kept falling for it.

I went to court on the charges and was put into an open custody place. It was more of a group home than a prison. You had to be up at a certain time, eat at this time, do chores when they tell you to, go to bed when they tell you. It wasn't that bad. It was dependable, anyway.

When I got out of there I was charged again, this time for trafficking in weapons. I was holding them for a friend and I took the blame rather than turn my friend in.

I went back into custody but this time it was secure custody, which was not good. It really was a jail although they didn't call it that. Some kids were in there for years, for really serious crimes. There was a school in the place and you had to attend. I liked the art class there. We decorated T-shirts and I liked that. The teacher said I did well with that.

I was in there for a few months. Then I was put on house arrest for more months. It was pretty crap. I couldn't go out by myself. I couldn't go to any of the places I liked. Dad wasn't happy because I was staying with him and he had to take time off work to supervise me sometimes. I just put in the time, mostly playing video games and doing some home schooling.

In grade ten I went to an alternative school but was kicked out for fighting. People there were being disrespectful to me, talking down to me, putting me down.

There was no place left for me to go to school. If I wanted an education, I'd have to make myself do it in my own house, so that's what I did. I only have three credits left to go, then I will graduate.

In February I got drunk with some people and we went out and robbed kids on the street. We were caught, of course, and convicted. I pled guilty to armed robbery.

I got sent to the most secure youth facility around here. It was hard to be away from my family, locked in a cell. I had to wear a prison uniform. I couldn't wear my own clothes. I didn't fight in there though. The guards kept a close eye on us and the penalties for fighting were severe, like getting thrown in the hole, so I didn't fight.

I became a reader instead. I'd never spent any time

reading before but I started in prison. They had an okay school and a pretty good little library, so I just read and read, book after book after book. My favorite? Crime books!

After a month or so, I got used to the routine of the facility. They had different levels they put you on, depending on your behavior. If you were on a high level you could earn canteen points by doing extra chores and use those to buy things like chips, pop, candy bars or body wash.

I got out of prison early because my behavior was good. Now I have five years of probation to do. If I mess up during those years, I'll go back behind bars. Simple as that.

Going forward, I'll finish up my high-school credits in a couple of months. I'm working two jobs now. One as a laborer in a factory and one job at a flower company. One day I'd like to open a clothing company. I'm also interested in geology and goldsmithing. I'll end up doing something interesting.

My life would have been easier if I'd hung around different kids from the beginning. If I had hung around kids who liked to do things instead of just prove how tough they were, then I would have done interesting, positive things too. There was always so much fighting around me. I just decided that fighting was the thing to do. My parents tried and tried to help me, but I never listened.

Taking Steps ...

For yourself

Before we try new things, we have to believe we have the right to try them. We have to be able to picture ourselves trying them. Is there something you have not had the confidence to believe you could try? Imagine yourself doing it, then take a step toward it.

For others

We could all use some help calming down. Could your student council, guidance department, phys ed department or a teacher sponsor anger management and meditation workshops at your school, open to everyone?

If you're a kid who's reading this, think about your future before you do anything stupid.

If you're an angry kid like me, start reading books, any books that interest you. When someone makes you want to punch them, take out your book and walk away and sit and read. It will calm you down and take your head to a better place. Even if you get in trouble for walking out of class, it's better than getting in trouble for hitting someone. No teacher with a brain in her head is going to slam you for sitting in the hall, reading a book.

A Sister's Story

I'm the oldest of three girls. My youngest sister is the one who was murdered. She was the first one of us to decide to have a baby. She was pregnant with her first child when she was murdered.

I was thirty-three when it happened. The killer was sixteen and from a wealthy white family. He grew up in a nice suburb in a beautiful home in a neighborhood full of multi-million-dollar homes. He got good grades. This was not someone with disadvantages.

He loved guns. He was too young to buy a gun on his own so he got some identification from an older man and used it to get a special card that would allow him to buy a gun—a gun-owner's ID card. This card came to his house in the mail. His parents found it first and took it to their lawyer, who had gotten their son out of trouble before. The lawyer could have destroyed it or turned it over to the police. Instead he locked it in his office and then went on vacation.

The offender who murdered my sister wanted this gun-owner's ID back. He broke into the lawyer's office. He couldn't get into the safe where the ID card was because it was locked, but in the lawyer's unlocked desk was a .357 magnum gun. That was the gun the offender used to kill my sister and her husband and their unborn baby.

The killer didn't know my sister or her husband. He just picked them at random. They were waiting to move into their new house and were staying, temporarily, in a town house that my parents had bought to retire in. The house was across the street from the police station. He wanted to do the killing under the nose of the police, to taunt them.

This offender was surrounded by adults who knew better, who could have stopped him, but who kept bailing him out of the trouble he got himself into.

His parents are professional people, well-educated pillars-of-society types, but they were in denial about how serious their son's problems were and they were easily

Mad as Hell

Anger is an emotion, but it also affects us physically. When we are angry, our amygdala — part of our brain's temporal lobe — decides if we should flee or fight. The amygdala makes that decision quickly, before we get a chance to think about it rationally. We can end up acting first and thinking later. Our adrenal glands flood our body with adrenaline and cortisol. Blood flows to our muscles, our temperature rises, our blood pressure rises and our heart rate increases. All this gives us the burst of energy and power we feel when we are angry.

When we get angry regularly, the systems in our body adjust to make chronic anger our new normal. We feel we are always on edge and ready to strike because we are — our brain has rewired itself to be constantly ready to lash out.

Chronic anger disrupts the body's natural system and can lead to high blood pressure, increased acne, head-aches, digestive issues, problems sleeping and even heart attacks.

We can talk ourselves into feeling angry. Sit by yourself one day when you are feeling calm and good. Imagine a situation that will get you angry. Notice the changes in your body. Now remind yourself that you are just telling yourself a story and think about something that makes you happy.

It may take a bit of practice, but you will be able to notice that you can lead your body's systems back to a state of relaxation.

This is good news. Our minds are strong and we can teach them. We don't have to allow our emotions to be a slave to the actions of others. We can learn to choose how we want to respond.

The benefits of mindful relaxation are such that many schools are building meditation into the school day. This reduces students' stress and makes it easier for them to learn.

manipulated by him. They bailed him out of one violent situation after another.

That doesn't excuse him. He still made his own choices. At sixteen we have enough messages about what is good behavior and what is not good to know right from wrong.

He knew right from wrong. With his parents bailing him out all the time, he learned that doing wrong brought no consequences. They taught him he could do what he liked.

My sister's murder turned me into an activist against violence. I work with troubled kids and help with restorative justice, ways for the young offender who has done the crime to try to repair some of the damage they did.

I meet often with groups of young people in trouble with the law. I tell them about my sister. I ask each young person, "Whatever you did to get arrested, what could you have done differently, that day, to keep yourself from doing the crime?"

And they have an answer! "I wouldn't have hung out with so and so," or, "I wouldn't have gone to that place," or, "I could have walked away instead of losing my cool."

To the young people reading this book I'd like to say that getting caught when you are doing something wrong can be good for you. It can shape you into someone who will make better choices next time.

Pay attention to how you are feeling. If you are feeling angry or alienated, or if you know someone is in that state, get help. Ask for help. If the first adult you ask doesn't help you, ask another, and keep asking, because you deserve it.

You don't have to become someone you're not in order to have a good life and not hurt others. Making even small, healthier changes can have a big, positive impact in your life. Find what interests you, what talents you have and pursue them in a positive way. You'll be amazed at how much better your life will be in a very short period of time.

Anita, 18

Statistics Canada's National Clearinghouse on Family Violence says that only 36 percent of female victims ever call the police on their male abusers. Half the women in battered women's shelters bring children with them. On any given night in Canada, 2,500 kids are sleeping in these shelters.

When girls witness their fathers or father figures beating on their moms, they begin to believe this is normal in a relationship. Boys who witness this learn that violence is the way to be a man. Often, boys with violent fathers will grow up to be violent husbands, unless they really work at making different choices. Girls with violent fathers often end up with violent boyfriends, unless they are able to really work at believing they deserve a whole lot better.

I grew up in a small town. Like, very small. Almost not a town at all. I hated it there. I didn't fit in at school and there were no other options because there was no place else to go.

The kids at school called me all kinds of vile racist names. I don't want to repeat what they called me. They were all white. The whole town was white. My mom was born in the Philippines so I looked different and the kids never let me forget it. The teachers knew this was going on but they didn't do anything to stop it.

It wasn't just that I looked different. I felt different, like an outsider. Maybe other kids there felt like outsiders too, but I never knew about it.

This really was a small town and there was nothing to do, no way out, no public transportation to get away. There were no clubs to join. It was just a grind. I went to school not very regularly.

My parents were really something. My mom was not around. She left when I was very little and went to live with someone else, a boyfriend. I didn't like to visit her. She was really moody. One time I said I didn't want to visit her and she called the cops on me. I told the cops I wanted to stay with my dad. Mom told me she didn't love me anymore.

Mom has another daughter. I have a sister. She's eight years older than me. Mom left her back in the Philippines and sent money to her family to look after her, only they didn't. When my sister finally came to Canada, her hair was all chopped off because she had lice and they didn't want to spend the money to treat it. She came without any clothes, nothing.

My dad was in a, let's say, alternative economy. As a kid I would see all these boxes of electronic stuff come into the house that I'm pretty sure was stolen. He'd sell the stuff then steal more.

Like, when I was a kid I wanted an MP3 player for my birthday. I was in the car with Dad and his friend. Dad's friend went into the store, came out with my MP3 player under his sweater and hid it under the seat where I was sitting. He was a bad dude. He later went to jail for drunk driving.

I don't know what the other kids in my school were going through at home and I certainly didn't tell them what I was going through. I in no way felt normal or like one of them.

I got into—what else?—drugs. Very young. In grade

?

- What are some reasons kids at your school might feel like outsiders?
- Anita spent three months in a mental health ward after suffering a drug-induced psychosis. What might that be like? What could drugs do to a person?

six I started drinking and smoking weed. More weed than booze because weed is easier for kids to get in a small town. It was just around. I only got booze when I was able to steal it from my grandparents.

In grade seven I took magic mushrooms. Just a tiny bit, the size of my pinkie nail. I didn't even get high, but I got suspended for five days. The reason I got caught was because the girl who brought them to school started running around like a fool, saying she was seeing things. I got ratted out.

That was the same year a kid came to my house with a gun and dared me to pull the trigger. I held the gun and pointed it but then I put it down. I felt like I could do too much with that gun and it would not be good. So I put it down. I don't know where he got it. Probably from his dad.

I got kicked out of my regular high school for almost never going and for being high all the time. I got sent to an alternative high school and learned practical things like how to silkscreen T-shirts. That's where I met my boyfriend.

Looking back, I see now that he was very secretive. I didn't know anything about him, not even his real age. I was fourteen and he said he was seventeen but he was really twenty-five. He was really violent and abusive to me but I excused a lot because I was lonely. Also, I'd grown up around violent men, so I thought that was normal.

The first warning sign I had was when he trapped me in the bathroom and yelled at me for something he thought I did wrong. He used to put his face right up against mine and yell and scream and spit at me and then he'd grab my hair and bang my head if he thought I wasn't listening to him hard enough. I thought it was my fault, that I had done things so wrong that I made this person so mad that he wanted to hurt me. Not just hurt me. He tried to kill me. More than once.

Things were bad at home and at school. I ran away when I was fourteen and went to live with my abusive boyfriend in a city an hour away. We lived in a trap house, which is just a house someone rents and a lot of people go there and do drugs. I started doing cocaine there.

I did a lot of cocaine and one day I did some cocaine that was mixed with poison or something and I ended up in a mental ward for three months. I had psychosis. It's like the drug would not leave my brain.

The cops were in and out of my life as a kid. They would come to the house because neighbors complained about shouting and screaming, or they would be around because of drugs. I never felt they were on my side. My dad, because of the way he made money, always wanted to avoid the police and I took that as my philosophy too. If I'd thought differently, maybe I would have asked them for help when I was being beaten, and maybe they would have given it.

That's in the past. I go to an alternative school in a small city. I can't function in a mainstream school with a

Signs You May Be in an Abusive Relationship

- He wants to know where you are all the time, who you are with and what you are doing.

- He is often critical of your appearance, behavior and words.

- He needs endless reassurance that you respect him and are not looking around for somebody better. You never know what is going to offend him and you find yourself watching your words and walking on eggshells so that you don't hurt his feelings.

- He demands things from you that he has no right to demand — your money, obedience, unwanted sexual behavior.

- He wants you all to himself, limiting your contact with family and other friends by ridiculing them, claiming they don't like him, forbidding you to contact them or making it so uncomfortable for you when you do that it begins to feel not worth the trouble. Your world gets smaller.

- He practices emotional blackmail: "If you loved me you would (or wouldn't) ..."

- He puts his hands on you in anger.

If you think you are in an abusive relationship, get help. It will not get better on its own. This does not mean that your boyfriend is a bad person. It means that he is dealing with his own emotions in a way that puts you at risk. Tell someone. Call your local women's shelter for counseling, or tell someone else you trust.

lot of teachers talking at me and expecting me to remember what they say. I learn best when I can read something on my own and then ask questions if I have any. Three years ago I had just three credits. Now I'm almost ready to graduate. I just have to pass a test on a science course and then I'll have that credit too.

I don't have any contact with the boyfriend who tried to kill me. He's probably doing the same thing to some other girl. If I go to the police about him they'll probably say, "You can't prove it," or "You were both doing drugs so you're both bad." Maybe he'll overdose and die. Then he won't be a threat to anyone ever again.

I've been staying at a youth shelter for some time now. The staff there know what I've been through and they keep feeding me positive messages, like my past is not my future. Soon I'll move into a more independent living situation. I play guitar and paint and like to hang out with friends. Yes, I have friends now! One friend kept asking me to smoke weed with her. I said, "Ask me again and we're not friends anymore." So she stopped asking.

I try not to go back to that small town where I grew up. It reminds me of how lonely I was and of how much time I spent in my room, smoking weed and feeling bad.

You know, I just wanted people not to treat me like shit every day so that I wouldn't feel like shit about myself.

Taking Steps ...

For yourself

Anita excused a lot of the warning signs her boyfriend gave out because she was lonely. Loneliness can affect our judgment. Are you ever lonely? What can you do to feel better in these times?

For others

Find the nearest shelter for abused women and children in your area. Help them by gathering and donating soap, pajamas, underwear and toys.

Post the warning signs for abusive partners in the school, especially in the girls' washrooms.

Maddie, 16

"The horse didn't trust me any more than I trusted him. Then I learned about his story."

Sexual assault victims are still too often revictimized by the justice system. They may not be believed. They may be accused of "asking for it." They may have their movements questioned, their sobriety questioned, and their choice of clothing questioned. The system can make a victim start to blame herself or himself for something that is never their fault.

Sexual assault help lines and crisis centers can provide advocates for victims of sexual violence.

My dad is an alcoholic and that made him abusive to us. He's hit us. He's said things to me like, "I hate your guts," and "I'd happily trade you for a case of beer." When we were younger he'd put us in his car and drive away drunk with us, saying he was going to kill us.

To fathers like that, I'd like to say, "Don't be surprised one day if your daughter hits you back."

Dad drank so much it gave him a stroke. I was fourteen when this happened. He could still say the same mean things but his body couldn't hit the way it used to, which made him act like a caged tiger, a whole new level of mean.

Mom tried to keep him at home for a year after the

144

stroke. She got him to counseling. She really tried. He wouldn't stop drinking and he wouldn't stop being abusive so she finally had him removed by the police. He went to a homeless shelter. He's still drinking.

When he would abuse me I started cutting myself because I didn't know what else to do.

My brother is not doing well. While the abuse was going on, he bottled it all up inside him but it's all coming out now. He's been arrested a lot, for theft, for fighting, for dangerous driving on a dirt bike, breach of conditions, on and on.

It wasn't just Dad who abused me. My first boyfriend raped me and there's another guy who finally got convicted for sexually harassing me when I was fourteen.

I was taken out of my mom's home because of the abuse and put into a group home. There were boys and girls in this group home. Boys slept on one side, girls on the other. You were not supposed to go to the side that was not yours.

This guy in the house was really sexually aggressive with me. I'd tell him to back off but he wouldn't. He came into the girls' section and into my room and was trying to rape me. So I slugged him. Hard.

The staff called the police and I was arrested and charged with assault. Nothing happened to the boy. He wasn't even punished for being on the girls' side. He got off scot-free.

I felt like I was being punished for saying no. The police cuffed me. They put me in the back of a cop car and took me to jail.

I wasn't allowed to keep my bra on in jail! They said I might use it to hang myself. Who hangs themselves with their bra? All my life I'd been abused by men and now these cops wanted me to sit in a cell, with no power, with all these armed men around, with no bra on. It felt like they were taking away an extra layer of protection I had.

The worst part was feeling like I was being punished for defending myself. The assault charge against me stuck.

?

• Maddie was afraid of the horse when she first met him. She could have decided to stay afraid and drop out of the program. What do you think helped her push through that fear? What helps you push through the fear of doing new and scary things? What sometimes holds you back from pushing through?

I'm now in a diversion program and I have to write the attacker a letter of apology.

Can you believe that? They are making *me* apologize to *him*!

I'm going to do it, only so I don't get charged with breach of conditions and so the charge of assault will be taken off my record.

I think I'm getting some money from victims' compensation for one of the other attacks and I'm going to spend it on horse therapy.

There is a horse farm near here run by a woman who does horse therapy with kids,

> "You gain strength, courage and confidence by every experience in which you really stop to look fear in the face. You are able to say to yourself, 'I have lived through this horror. I can take the next thing that comes along.' You must do the thing you think you cannot do."
>
> — Eleanor Roosevelt, *You Learn by Living: Eleven Keys for a More Fulfilling Life*

veterans, abused women, abused men—anybody who has had trouble in their lives and needs help.

I've been there before, to help me deal with the abuse.

See, I'm not good around a lot of people because I have bad anxiety. I got kicked out of school because my anxiety would not let me function in a classroom. Especially when I would have to be around groups of guys, and you can't avoid groups of guys in high school. They're everywhere. I would get aggressive and want to fight them because I never knew when they would give me problems. I was cutting and fighting and the administration asked me to leave the school.

My marks were good, but people are not always good for me.

Horses are different.

When I first started working with a horse I was very afraid of it because I didn't know what to do and the horse was so much bigger than I was.

The horse didn't trust me any more than I trusted him. Then I learned about his story. He was a rescued horse. His other owner had starved him and beaten him. When he came to the therapy farm he was in really bad shape.

The lady who runs the farm put me together with that horse so we could learn how to trust again together. We could heal each other.

I didn't ride him straight off. We did ground exercises. I would push him a ball and he learned to push it back to me. I learned how to walk him, how to groom him and how to put his saddle on.

All the time I was cleaning the tack or walking the horse, I found myself talking to the woman who runs the place, telling her things I'd never told anyone. It seemed easier to talk with the horse there, easier to be honest.

When I'm with the horse, I have to leave my anxiety at the gate because the horse will pick up on it and also become anxious. So I've learned how to manage my anxiety better.

The lady here took me for some sessions for free but she can't do that all the time, so I'm glad that victims' services helped me get money so that I can get some more help.

I'm back living with my mom now, trying to do the rest of high school from home. Mom has bad arthritis and can

Taking Steps …

For yourself

Spend time with a non-human creature. Feed the birds, pat a dog, scoop some kitty litter, volunteer at a shelter. Give yourself the joy of being around other creatures.

For others

Cigarette butts are poisonous to animals and birds. Organize a butt pick-up on a street or in a park. Give non-humans a cleaner place to live.

hardly walk so she has a small health pension. The place we live in is out in the country. It has cheap rent but we don't have a car so that's sometimes a problem. In the winter, especially, we get sort of stuck there.

I like reading and staying active and working with animals. If I can get my high school done, maybe I can have a career with animals somehow.

I feel like I am finally starting to put all the abuse behind me.

Voice of Experience: Hilary, 39

My dad beat up his girlfriend and made us kids watch. My mom was abused by her alcoholic dad. She did the best she could. I don't want to be like my parents.

My first boyfriend was in and out of prison. He's currently inside. Lots of violence from him. It didn't really surprise me when he started abusing me. That's what I grew up with. That's what men did.

I had three kids with him and was working a full-time job. I went out on the streets with a girlfriend and sold drugs to make more money. We got caught, of course. I had to do six years for that—three in custody and three out on bail. That was like a jail sentence too. I could only go out certain hours, had to submit to pee tests, all that.

I am now married to a man who is in prison. We corresponded for three years before I finally went to the prison to meet him in person. When I told people I was going to marry him, everyone said, "What are you doing? You don't know him. What kind of relationship can you have over the phone?" But he is my soulmate. I've never been happier. He's even helped me quit smoking. He had a rough life but has become a new person in prison, kind and gentle.

Every time I go to see him in prison I get strip-searched. I have medical issues, so am on medical marijuana and Percocet for pain. I always get the attention of the drug dog. I have to bring in letters from the doctor to let them know that the drugs are legal. I don't bring them into the prison but they are in my system.

Still, the whole thing is humiliating and degrading. I try to get myself ready for it, but there have been so many times I've run out of the search room, crying that I'm not a criminal. But the guards are the boss and they let you know it.

My kids are teenagers now. Their biological dad is a heroin addict. They have all met my husband who is in prison and they like him. One of my children wants my husband to adopt her.

One of my children is having a rough time with everything. She's getting into trouble. She had to go into a group home because she was running away so much. My mother had to go in front of a judge and tell what my daughter was doing, that we couldn't properly supervise her, and she needed to go into a group home.

Because of my charges, there were many things I could never do with my kids. Like, I could never take them to Disneyland because crossing a border with a criminal record—well, you can't.

If I could do things over again, I never would have gotten in trouble with the law. Some mistakes you have to keep paying for.

If you're in trouble, reach out for help. There's always help, even if it doesn't come from the first person you ask, or the first ten people. There's always help. You are not alone. There are organizations that will help you. Pick up the phone.

I was embarrassed that I was in a relationship with a man who beat me, like there was something wrong with me because I chose a violent man. I have so many scars on my face from him, and the emotional scars are even worse.

Jeremy, 17

"Court gives you the feeling that you can never make up for what you did, that you're just bad forever."

Ah, the joy of going for a walk by yourself, strolling through the world in a way that you choose, going this way or that on a whim, with a bit of money in your pocket to buy a small snack, one that you pick out from a place you select.

It's a simple pleasure, yet one that is denied to many people around the world. It is denied to women and girls in countries where they are not allowed to be out by themselves. It is denied to people who live in war zones or in communities where the high levels of violence make casual walks too dangerous.

For those in hospitals, nursing homes and behind bars, the walks we get to take are walks they are no longer able to experience.

I lived with my dad for the first couple years of my life. Then my parents separated. After that I lived with Mom for a few years. I went into Children's Aid care when I was seven. I was with a foster family for a year, then went to live with my grandmother from the time I was eight until the time I was twelve.

At twelve I had to go into anger management in another foster home for a year. After that they put me

?

• The treatment center where Jeremy lives will have no legal right to hold him past his eighteenth birthday. Is he ready to be a free man? What does he need to learn in order to be ready?

into a treatment center. I've been there ever since.

The treatment center is a big place with a wall around it and many houses and other buildings inside the wall.

I live in a house with nine or ten other kids, like a group home. I have my own room. No other kids can come into my room.

There's a lot of limitations on what I can do. I have to ask permission for everything. I have to ask permission to get a drink and to go to the washroom.

Sometimes I feel trapped. I think I've become institutionalized.

My house is all boys. Most of the houses at the center are for boys. There's two for girls, maybe three. There's a school on the grounds that's just for kids at the center. Some kids go to local schools. I go at the center. It's a small school with small classes.

The other kids in the center are like me, not good with the justice system. They have ongoing issues with the law. Some don't have families to live with anymore or they're not allowed to live with their families. It's none of my business why they're at the center so I don't ask.

I get along with some of them. Some need the same kind of help as me, with anger management.

Sometimes we get to go on supervised outings. We've been to a baseball game, an amusement park, a skate park and swimming. We have to stay within sight of a staff. We have some say in what we do or where we go—like, we can give suggestions—but we don't always get to choose.

There are some foster homes out in the world where you can go out to Walmart by yourself. Two and a half years ago, I was in one of those, but I got into trouble with the law again and they moved me back here to the higher supervision home.

When it's a school holiday you have to be out of bed and "on the floor," which means in program, by 11 a.m. Then you can go back to your room. During the school year, you have to be up at seven for breakfast, tidy your room and leave the house and walk across the grounds to school.

"Thinking [in a new way] is like a walk in the forest. The first time through, it's difficult, you break branches out of your way, your feet push down on the moss. The more often you walk through the same area, the easier it becomes. Eventually you have a trail to follow, a trail of your own making. Thinking works the same way. The first time you are thinking about something new, it's difficult. The more often you think about the same thing, the easier it becomes. Your brain creates networks that allow you to think the same thought over and over again. It follows the path you created. Pretty soon it seems like there is no other way of walking, or of thinking."

— Harold R. Johnson, *Firewater: How Alcohol Is Killing My People (and Yours)*

School starts at 9:15. You have to always walk in sight of staff.

Having to always be within sight of a staff truly sucks. I've been in there for so long. I hate having to ask for a drink or to go to the bathroom. Staff say I have to do this so they know where I am at all times. It's a precaution, they say. They have to know I haven't left the house.

Bedtime is 9 p.m. or 10 p.m. You can earn the later bedtime if you have a day with no or few issues. We used to have a point system, where you earn points for chores and good behavior then spend the points on late bedtimes and privileges but they took that system away. I don't know why they changed it.

I get an allowance of $10 a week. They have to give it to me. It's part of Children's Aid. The center can't take it away, even if I break all the rules.

If you damage something in the house you have to pay for what you broke. You can save up your allowance or you can do chores. They pay you $3.50 an hour for things like cutting the grass, washing the windows, extra chores like that. If you haven't broken anything you can still earn money and have it on outings but you can't have money in the house. The staff keeps it for you.

I've been on damages before. It takes a long time to pay for things when you only make $3.50 an hour and you can only do that if the staff have chores they feel like hiring you to do.

It is very frightening going to court. Even though I had a lawyer to explain things to me. I was fourteen when I went. Court gives you the feeling that you can never make up for what you did, that you're just bad forever.

I turn eighteen in a few months so they are soon going to try putting me into a less supervised foster home on the grounds. If they don't do that then I'll just go straight into independent living when I'm eighteen. The Children's Aid Society will give me a monthly allowance for a year or so but I'll be living on my own.

So, I'll be free at eighteen! I haven't been out in the

community on my own for such a long time. I almost don't know what I would do. There's so much I don't know how to do since I've been living in the treatment center for so long. I don't know how to shop for groceries or how to pay bills or cook or manage my life.

The court system put me on probation and part of that is I get a coach to help me sort out and plan my life. He picks me up at the center and we'll grab a slice of pizza and talk about things I need to know. He's helping me get a job in a bike shop. I like working with my hands on

Taking Steps ...

For yourself

Go for a walk by yourself. Decide for yourself where to go. Buy a small snack of your choosing. While you do this, think of all those who, right at this moment, can't.

Ask some independent adults what they are responsible for. Find out what you'll need to know, such as how to file your income taxes, how to avoid being scammed, how to make and stick to a budget, how to cook and clean up after yourself. Find out where you can go to learn these things.

For others

Pass your knowledge on! Learn to make a fantastic casserole, then have friends over for a casserole-making party. Invite someone to join you to talk about one of the things you will need to know, like how easy it is to get into trouble with credit cards.

cars and bikes. When I was really young I used to help my uncle fix cars.

I have a bike at the treatment center. I've had it for years. I ride it around the grounds when there is a staff who wants to go with me on another bike.

It will be very different when I turn eighteen and can ride my bike anywhere I want to at any time and on my own.

I try not to think about the negative things in my past. I guess a lot of my anger problems are because of my dad but it doesn't really help me to dwell on that. I need to build up the inside of myself. The coaching helps a lot with that. It's helping me figure out how to do the things I want to do for myself.

My family has had a lot of pain. We are Métis, so I wear a Native Pride hat to remind me of my heritage and our strength.

You need to make the best of a situation, no matter how hard it is at the moment. Try to find something good for yourself in it, and if you can't, just try to get through it without getting yourself into more trouble.

Voice of Experience: Fletcher, 25

I came from a neighborhood in the city where it was bad for a lot of people. My mom was drunk a lot. I was in and out of foster care, like, twenty-one times. There were times when I did live with my mom but it was like I didn't even know her. She gave me all kinds of abuse—physical, mental—all because of her drinking.

My grandfather—Papa—was an alcoholic too but he also worked full-time on the lake. Nana worked in the Band office. I remember being five or six years old and staying with them, running around the reserve with the other kids, feeling very free and safe.

Papa and Nana were both in the residential schools. The abuse that they were given there messed them up.

It messed up a lot of people. There was no help for them after. They didn't learn how to be good parents. My mom paid a price for those schools. She was in and out of foster care too. All of her brothers and sisters were taken away.

My grandfather's ancestors built the community. He can trace them way back in history.

I have two sisters and two brothers. They have a lot of the same problems that I have. The way I was treated growing up—I just didn't learn any better. When I was seven I was cooking for them, getting them up and dressed to go to school. Then when we got home, my mom would hurt us for no reason. By the time I was nine years old I was going around fighting everyone. I didn't know how else to be. We had no toys. Our house was so messy. I didn't know how to help myself.

At ten and a half I remember driving my drunk uncle around the reserve. At twelve I was in a gang. When I was eleven and a half, someone took me aside and said, "If you're ever stuck for money, I'm going to teach you to look after yourself. I'm going to teach you how to steal cars."

All these foster homes—I'd get put in with complete strangers. Most were white. A few were Native. Me and my sisters were always together in care. My younger brother didn't get to stay with us. He grew up okay. He graduated high school and has two jobs. My other siblings still live with addictions.

I ran away when I was, I think, thirteen. I was in a desperate situation on the reserve with my mom. Her drinking was just so bad. One day, I grabbed everything I could, packed a bag, stole the rest of my mom's liquor and her boyfriend's marijuana and left. I had to wait for the ferry, so I slept underneath a truck, by the big tires so no one would see me. I got on the ferry, stole a vehicle and drove all the way to the city. I parked the vehicle in a hospital parking lot and walked and walked. My oldest sister was living there so I called her and she told me how to find her.

I showed my sister the stuff I stole. She showed me how to deal the stuff and sell it on the street.

By the age of thirteen I was on hard drugs—cocaine, other things. I got into a gang. My mind wasn't set right. I was too young. But the gang and my siblings made me feel wanted and loved instead of having to run away from foster homes down streets I didn't know.

There were consequences to what I was doing, for sure. I got put in jail. They'd put me away then let me go again, back out to the streets.

The streets are a hard place to live. The youth jail was better than the streets. Sometimes I broke into cars so that the police would take me back to jail.

Jail was strange, because I felt safe in the cell but it also made me act out. The feelings of neglect—it made me feel that nobody wanted me. I'd get into fights with staff and the guards, then I'd get out of jail and just fight for the hell of it.

I was scared the first time I went to jail. The first week, really, was pretty rough. I didn't eat because I wanted to be home. I started gambling to get money for the commissary to get junk food since that's all I felt like eating.

That's how I got started in all that. I got older and they sent me to federal penitentiaries. I got stabbed, shot, moved around to different places, jails and prisons. I wouldn't want my life to be lived by anybody.

I might have had an easier road if I'd been put in with family members when I was a kid instead of jumping around with foster care.

My dad wasn't even in my life until I was thirteen. My mom went through drug treatment twice in order to get us back with her.

It's not a straight road, but I've been doing good. What kept me doing good was being involved in traditional practices, like powwow, sun dances, sweat lodges. You can't do these things if you are on drugs because that is disrespectful to the ancestors. So I'd get clean in order to do the ceremonies.

I know my language—Ojibwe—and I want my children to know that they are a part of the great Anishinaabe people.

There was so much bad stuff when I was growing up, but there was a lot of good times too. Living on the reserve and living off the land up north. I went hunting to put meat in the fridge. I loved checking the traplines in the winter and in the spring going in the canoe for miles and miles. Some days we might not get anything but we'd just go out the next day and try again. My grandfather would fish. We would fillet the fish to hand out to the Elders. We'd bring back elk and moose and deer and duck and geese, all in season. On treaty days, everyone would gather for a feast.

Many from my generation don't keep up the traditions because of what they've been through in life, but I'm trying to. I got my daughter into fancy dress dancing and my boy into grass dancing. They both have their Indian names.

Right now I'm on probation. I've got a few months left. Breaches, mostly. I got out of prison in November. The law is doing their job by trying to keep the streets safe, but they also hurt people.

As a young teen, it felt powerful when I had money from drug sales. I wanted to be a gangster to feel even more powerful. But I hurt so many people over the years who didn't need to be hurt. That comes back to haunt me.

My main responsibility now is to my kids and my community. There are so many funerals to go to. One of my young cousins was pulled from the river. Just this month I had to bury five people, from suicide or other early death.

My advice for kids now? Whatever is going on for you at home, find someone to talk to. Keep looking until you find someone you can trust. You tell them what is going on with you, let them help you, and then, when you are strong, you help someone else.

Fred, 18

"That really had an impact on me, that I could be the sort of guy who could be that brutal."

A teenager's brain is still growing, even if their body seems full-sized. If alcohol is put into this growing brain, it can damage the way the brain works. Teens can end up with poor memory, impaired ability to move and clumsy coordination. Those who start drinking before age fifteen are four times more likely to develop a physical dependency on alcohol than those who don't take their first drink until they are twenty-one (Foundation for a Drug-Free World).

I grew up in a small city. I still live with my parents. Mom came to Canada thirty years ago from Scotland. She works as a hairdresser.

Dad was taken out of the workforce. He was in prison for twenty years. He got out and then two years later, I was born.

Dad went to prison for murder when he was seventeen. He was out drinking with one of his friends. There was an incident and he beat his friend to death. Dad was in three different prisons. He had a rough time in those places. He doesn't talk about it much. He's alive and that's all that matters.

I was supposed to graduate last June but I didn't. My

whole life, I didn't like school. I got so many suspensions in elementary school. It was probably grade seven when I started skipping.

I had a tough family life and I'd take all that tension to school and be mean to teachers and other kids, and then I'd get suspended for it.

My parents are raging alcoholics. When they drink they treat each other like shit and they treat me like shit. That's why I don't really drink.

Mom's been in and out of jail all my life, usually for being drunk or fighting while she was drunk or driving while she was drunk. The booze has affected her health so badly. She had a stroke because of it and now she has seizures. Doesn't stop her drinking, though, and it doesn't stop my dad.

I've moved out twice. Once was with a friend and once was with an older brother. Neither worked out and I had no money and no options so I moved back into my parents' house.

I've been arrested a few times, like four times. The first was when I was thirteen. I burnt some kid with a cigarette. I can actually say I was bullying the kid. I bullied many kids. I once almost made some kid kill himself.

That really had an impact on me, that I could be the sort of guy who could be that brutal. I sort of stepped back and looked at myself, and I didn't like what I saw.

It didn't stop me though. I didn't know how to turn it around.

I was arrested again when I was thirteen for assault with a weapon. I had to go to court and I had my lawyer say I didn't do it even though I was guilty. I'm not proud of it, but I got off the charge.

When I was fourteen I was arrested for public intoxication. I was drunk and flopping, staggering all down the street. The police picked me up and let me sleep it off in the drunk tank.

Two weeks after that I had an MDMA [ecstasy] blackout. I guess I was fifteen then. I was completely wrecked on MDMA. The details are still fuzzy. I remember knowing the police were coming for me so I took off down the street. The police pulled their car up alongside me. They asked me my name. I told them and they said, "You're under arrest for assaulting your mother."

I didn't even know. I'd blacked out. According to my dad I was all hung-over from MDMA and then I took some more MDMA and that took me right out of myself. Mom was drunk and abusive and came at me and I was all strung out and I flipped out on her.

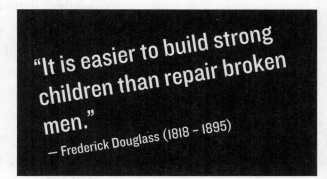

"It is easier to build strong children than repair broken men."
— Frederick Douglass (1818 – 1895)

Mom was often abusive to me when she was drunk and she usually got away with it. Not this time. I guess the lesson there is, "Don't hit someone who is on drugs. You never know what will happen."

The police arrested me for the assault and put me in a holding cell for twenty-four hours. Then I was shipped to another jail. They put me in handcuffs and shackles and I had to ride in a police wagon. I sat in court waiting for my bail hearing. I just sat with my head down because I felt so sick and scared and alone.

When I finally looked up, there was my mother's friend. She bailed me out and let me live with her for a little while. She was really strict. That was good for me even though I wasn't used to it and didn't know what to do with it. She taught me manners.

After I got out of jail for the assault I was okay for about a year. Then I went on an eleven-day binge with crystal meth and almost died. I was doing so much crystal meth back then. My weight is usually 160 but it went down to seventy-five pounds. I had scars all over my body from shooting up.

There was some bad stuff going on in my life at that

time. I was under stress from work. There was not much money in the house so my parents wanted me to work and help out. What kind of work could I get? I could sell drugs.

You buy a little bit and sell it for more than you bought it for. You use the profits to buy a little more and sell that for more, and on it goes. I made a lot of money selling drugs. Once I saved up $3000, but then I broke the big rule. Don't get high on your own supply! I started using again and got broke real fast.

The last time I was arrested was almost a year ago, some stupid thing over a cellphone. They gave me a diversion for that, so I didn't have to go to jail.

I turned eighteen a month ago. Now if I mess up I'll be charged as an adult and I really don't want that.

I've got thirteen high-school credits to go before I graduate. I want to get that done and then build something good with my life. I try to be really careful now so that I won't get into trouble. Life can throw stuff at you. You can be all innocent but at the wrong place at the wrong time and then it all goes bad. So I'm careful. I still go to trap houses sometimes to see friends but I make sure I have no drugs on me.

What really could have made the difference? If my parents were not alcoholics. If I didn't grow up in this city. All the high schools here know me as a stoner and a crackhead. I dug myself a big hole that I couldn't get out of.

What I want now is to finish school and start my life but do it in the right way. Some of my friends are fourteen and they have kids already. They don't know how to be fathers and their kids are going to pay for that. I don't want to hurt anyone anymore.

My father wants me to go up north with him and hunt our own food and live off the land but I'm not sure that would work out. What I'd really like to do is become an environmental scientist. That would be something useful and good and would help me pay the world back for all the bad I've done.

?

- Is there something you do or don't do that you would like to change but haven't been successful at yet? What do you think is holding you back?
- Fred's mother's friend was strict with him and taught him manners. Why does he think that was good for him?

A Mother's Story

My youngest son is in prison for murder.

We first heard that he was arrested when the police showed up with a warrant to search our house for evidence. The police refused to tell us anything and we thought maybe our son's friends had done something wrong. We went to a neighbor's house while the police searched and while we were there the news of our boy's arrest came over the television.

I could not believe this was happening, that my son was being charged with murder! I worked as a homecare provider and so often this boy would come with me to work to provide a little extra help for people, tidying their lawns, helping me clean their homes. He was gentle, he was kind, he was such a hard worker. Arrested for murder? This was not the kid I knew.

My son was known for helping people. He went to school one day and saw someone passed out in the alley. He couldn't leave until he was able to get the man some help. One of my neighbors was dealing with senility and my son saw him inappropriately dressed on the sidewalk. My son brought the old man to me because he knew that I would know what to do. My son was also involved with raising money for years and years so girls in Afghanistan could go to school. *That* was my son. How could he be charged with first-degree murder?

It's taken me five years to accept that he did it. His DNA was there. He did it. His lawyer says we may never

---

Taking Steps ...

For yourself

If you live with parents who abuse alcohol, get help for yourself. Attend a meeting of Al-Anon for family members of alcoholics to learn how to keep yourself well through the alcoholic's chaos.

For others

If you know of a kid who might be struggling with an addicted parent, be kind to them, even in small ways. Let them know you are on their side.

know the details of why because my son says he can't remember, but I needed to accept in my head that he did it so that I could be a mother to him in the here and now.

The things families have to deal with when their loved one goes to prison! They have to deal with community reaction in a way the person locked away in prison doesn't. I've known families who have to move because of the harassment they get from neighbors.

There is so much we know now that we wish we never had to know.

We learned about the incredible power the police have with search warrants. As soon as the warrant comes to your door, you no longer have ownership over your house or anything in it. I had a photograph of a rosebud that I had taken and I picked it up while the police search was on and the officer said, "Put that down! It's not yours now!"

My son was in jail but our family's home was surrounded by police tape. Police went through all our personal things. We had not done anything wrong but we were being treated like criminals and there was nothing we could do or say about it. We had to find somewhere else to stay until the police said we could go home.

Our son is lucky that he has us to put money in his commissary account. If you are in prison and have no one who will send you money, you are poor, poor, poor, because the prison provides very little in terms of the necessities and dignities of life.

The prison website has a list of what a family can send someone and what they can't. You can't send stamped envelopes, for example. You can't send birthday cards with sparkles or music or googly eyes.

My son was in a provincial jail for four years, waiting for his trial, going through the trial and then waiting for sentencing. He spent twenty-two hours every day locked in his cell when he wasn't sitting in a courtroom or in a court-house jail. He had no TV, very limited reading, very little access to outside air. We tried sending him a magazine subscription but he couldn't get it because it had staples in the spine and staples could be turned into weapons.

Now he is in a prison on the other side of the country from us, making it very difficult for us to visit him.

My son is a first-degree murderer but he is also someone who did good things in his life. He stopped some little kids from being bullied. He helped people who needed it. Even behind bars, he helps people. From when he assisted me in looking after people with dementia, he knows how to calm down prisoners who are not mentally well, and that makes the prison safer for everyone.

As a society we really are about revenge, not about caring and helping. Sometimes we all do things we don't think we are ever going to do, and sometimes that ends in a very, very bad result.

All of us are just one bad moment away from prison.

Kate, 21

"Mom kept disappearing."

It can take very little to improve someone's story. One caring adult in the life of a child. One caring teacher who recognizes the potential in a struggling student. One moment of kindness that shines through years of degradation and says to a child, "You are worth something."

It doesn't change things overnight, but over time, a child can stop believing the negative messages they have been given and start believing the new, positive ones. When we believe we are worthy of good things, it makes us want to do good things. When we feel we belong, it makes us want to contribute, and with every contribution, we feel stronger and kinder.

Wow. Where do I start? I've been in this city since I was five. I was in a larger city before that, in a rough part of that city. It's rough now and it was scary then. Even though I moved away from there when I was five, I kept on going back.

We moved because Mom needed to escape her lifestyle. She had friends in this city so we moved here.

My biological dad took off when Mom was in the hospital giving birth to me. He robbed Mom of everything she had. I slept in a dresser drawer for the first six months of my life because my father stole all the baby things Mom had collected for me, probably to sell for drugs.

Mom got involved with another man then. Stepdad. They got into selling crack. They were smoking it one day and got into a huge fight and that's when Mom decided to split.

At the time, I was really angry at Mom for moving us but now that I'm a mom I can see her point.

I grew up with Mom and one sister. I have two other siblings but they were adopted out because Mom was so young when she had them. I've never had a home I stayed in for very long. Mom was kicked out of her parents' home at a young age. She lived on the streets, got pregnant and had absolutely no idea of how to parent. She was an addict too. Any little thing would set her off.

I remember her having some job over one holiday season but not any other work. She had terrible back pain. From the time I can remember I'd walk on her back, massaging her back and listen to her cry that she couldn't handle the pain anymore.

Mom tried to teach us how to stay away from bad guys and was open about her addiction. I have a lot of hate in my heart for her, but I do understand her better than I used to. Her dad was an alcoholic and her mom had her own party days with drugs and clubs, and she made it clear to me once that she never liked my mother.

The lack from Mom's childhood carried over to my childhood. If we ever managed to get anything of value it ended up in the pawn shop when the fridge was empty. We always ate. There were many days when all we ate was toast with mayonnaise. Even if she was wasted she would somehow scramble up a dollar or two for a loaf of bread. I hated toast and mayonnaise then—I craved burgers!—but now I give Mom credit for doing what she could.

Mom had never been given love so she didn't know how to receive it from her own children. That was hard. She only ever once put her hands on me in anger though, and I deserved it. I got into a fight with a girl in the park. I was making fun of the girl's make-up, bullying her, and Mom was mad at me for that.

She didn't really hit me. She just swatted me on the behind. She said she was hit a lot when she was a kid and she did not want to treat me in the same way.

She scared me with her yelling though, and when she felt bad about herself she'd write on the mirrors, "I'm worthless." I was glad she didn't walk me to school because she didn't take care of herself. She was often dirty and messy. This was embarrassing to me because it made me feel we lived lower than others.

"We can't change prisons without changing society; we know that this is a long and dangerous struggle. But the more who are involved in it, the less dangerous, and the more possible it will be."
— Claire Culhane

She and Stepdad were never really over. He'd float in and out of our lives. Sometimes he would show up with a whole rack of clothes for us and I knew they were stolen but what could I do?

One day he came home with garbage bags stuffed with something. I thought it was new clothes. It turned out to be marijuana. I helped him and Mom weigh it out and package it to be sold. I thought it was just grass we were playing with, like lawn grass.

I changed schools twenty-five times. Some were the same school I'd go back to then leave then go back to again.

In grade five I remember going to four different schools. Each one was teaching at a different level, doing different things, some too easy for me and some too hard.

Here's something really nice. One of those fifth-grade teachers recognized me on a bus years later! She said hello to me and asked me how I was. She said she liked having me in her class. I floated away on that for a long time, so if she reads this, it meant a lot.

My sister is developmentally delayed. She's twenty-four but really more like a young teen. I've always been protective of her. I remember being in kindergarten and beating on much older kids who made fun of her.

I remember one kid being very mean to my sister. His parents were there and they told him, gently, to stop it and explained why it wasn't the right way to behave. I wanted to go home with those parents.

On one of my really dark days, I wanted to just disappear. I thought, "This is how Mom felt when she first picked up a crack pipe." I decided right then to never do drugs and I don't.

Mom would up and disappear a lot. She'd head back to that bigger city and disappear into the drug neighborhood. Sometimes she would take me and my sister with her. We would hang out with the girls who were working the street and I just wanted to be back in school.

Sometimes we would go to the food banks in the bigger city because we could get more food there. My biological father would let us use his address to register with them instead of paying child support. I remember being at Bio-Dad's place and he had all these girls' names and numbers written on his wall. I think now that he was pimping them. I decided to add my own doodles to the wall, since it seemed like it was okay to draw on that wall. He screamed at me and hit me and grabbed a cucumber and beat me with it. Well, I went crazy and beat him back with everything I could grab. I wanted so hard to hurt him and kill him.

That was the last time Mom made me go there. I have had no contact with him since that day. Someone told me he's in prison now, hooked up to liver machines and dying. Someone else told me he's living by the train tracks.

Mom kept disappearing. I would go and live with aunties. Any friend of Mom's was called Auntie. Most of

- Can you think of a time someone was unexpectedly kind to you? How did it change your day? Can you think of a time when you were unexpectedly kind to someone else? What prompted you to act that way? How did it make you feel? What can you build into your life to remind yourself that you add value to this world?

them were also on booze or drugs and I was in the way. Not that they weren't nice to me. They were. But it was not good, being around the things they did to make money.

All the adults around me were messed up so I decided to make my own decisions and I ran away.

I lived on the streets for a bit. How old was I? Twelve? There were so many years of this that they all run together. I slept where I could — laundromats were open all night — until I was picked up by the police and taken to a foster home.

I was there for a few weeks. The foster mom was great but I messed up. I had to change schools again and just couldn't manage it. I attacked people for anything I thought might be disrespect. The girls at the school found me strange and they'd throw stuff at me like pens. One day I couldn't take it. I picked up my whole desk and threw it at the ringleader. She flew back onto the floor and I got into a lot of trouble.

I went back to the foster home that day and Foster Mom said I was grounded. I said, "Do you know where I came from? You can't ground me!" She said, "Yes, I can, and you're grounded." So I accepted it. She wasn't afraid of me and she thought I was worth correcting.

I liked her but I couldn't go to that school so I ran away again. The police found me again and they put me into a group home. I arrived there late at night and was supposed to do registration in the morning. Some girls came into my room and threatened me, so I just walked out in the middle of the night.

It was cold and raining and my shoes had big holes. I just walked and walked and thought I should maybe just die right on the sidewalk.

Finally I came to the home of another one of my mom's friends, another "Auntie" who was doing okay. She let me come in and Children's Aid agreed that I could live with her. She made me go to school, do homework right after school, read for an hour every evening and then write about what I'd read. Her home was in a catchment area for a school I'd been to before and liked and they let me go there. I played on the volleyball team, something I always wanted to do but couldn't because we never had the money. (Once when Mom said we had no money for sports, I said, "We have the money for weed, why not for sports?" I don't think she had an answer.)

I was at this house for a year and doing well. Then Mom got herself together and the Children's Aid let her have me back. That lasted a couple of weeks until she had to go to the hospital for taking some bad acid. She also had a new boyfriend who was always trying to come into my room. Good job, Children's Aid. You sure found me a safe place that time! It happened other times too. Children's Aid would put me in homes where the woman had a boyfriend and the boyfriend was a creep. Doesn't Children's Aid have to find this stuff out before they let someone be a foster parent?

I got a lot of charges on me over the years. When I ran away, I stole food from the grocery store because I had no money and I was hungry. I got petty theft charges from those times, other small charges and some assault charges.

The first assault charge was for something stupid, stupid girl drama. Some kids said stuff on Facebook about someone I knew so we went down to their school. We were just going to scare them but things ended up getting out of hand and we all beat on this one girl. Then we tried to run but the teachers barricaded the doors so we couldn't escape. We were arrested and I had to sit in a jail cell for a lot of hours waiting to be processed.

Jail is awful. It's cold. You can't get warm. It smells bad. All these officers walk by your cell and no one tells you anything. You're nothing to them.

The next assault charge came when this guy I'd broken up with came right into my classroom when school was on and started saying nasty things about me, nasty things like what men would say to my mother when they were beating her.

I was up and out of my seat in a flash and started

smashing this guy. He tried to run and I kept on smashing him all over the school until the police could catch me and stop me.

It broke my heart that I had fallen into my mom's pattern.

I went to court and had to do volunteer work at a community center, scrubbing walls and cleaning toilets. It was all right. The staff were nice and they brought me food and said thank you like I was doing them a favor instead of being punished, which was kind and helped calm me.

I also had to do one-on-one counseling with a youth justice intervention program. That's what changed things for me.

Children's Aid workers were supposed to provide counseling but mostly they only seemed interested in telling me what I was doing wrong.

This counselor really listened to me. She made me feel like a person, and once I felt like a person, I could start to really think about what I wanted and did not want in my life.

I managed to graduate high school with honors and on time, with my age group. I did a two-year college course

---

Taking Steps ...

For yourself

We often believe the negative messages the world sends us about ourselves, such as, "You're just a bad kid," and "You'll never amount to anything." Make a list of those messages that affect you and try to figure out where they come from. Then deliberately replace them with positive images, such as, "I can learn how to focus," and "I have things to share that the world needs."

For others

Where can homeless young people go to get out of the rain in your community? Those who live on the street often have foot problems from spending their days and nights with wet feet. Clean dry socks are a big deal. Do a sock drive and set up a Free Sock Box at your school. You never know who might need them!

to work with at-risk youth and now I have a full-time job helping teen moms find their way in the world.

I have a baby, too, a son. His name is something I made up, something that is all his own. His father doesn't live with us, although we are working at having a good parenting relationship. My son and I have a little apartment in rent-geared-to-income housing and we are doing all right.

As a child, I never felt safe. I don't know how many times I sat in school wishing the bell would never ring because I was afraid to go home. I don't know how many times I stood before a judge, begging him to find me somewhere safe to live. I've been hurt and I've been violent,

Resilience

Resilience is the ability to bounce back when life knocks you down.

If you have resilience, or are resilient, mistakes and defeats still hurt you, but they don't define you. You will be able to see them as stepping stones to take you to where you want to go.

When you are resilient and someone's bad behavior hurts you, you are more easily able to say, "What is wrong with them that they acted this way?" rather than, "What is wrong with me that they acted this way?"

Resilience can be acquired and strengthened. Every time we fall off our bike and watch ourselves get back up on it and try again, skinned knees and all, we build resilience. Every time we watch ourselves keep our word, take care of our bodies, reach a little farther and take steps toward what we want, even with difficulties and obstacles, we build resilience.

Resilience is about looking for what we can control for ourselves in a bad situation. Life can be a mess. Things can happen to us that are not our fault and for which there will never be a truly just resolution. We can keep moving forward.

Viktor Frankl was in a concentration camp during World War II. He was starving, scared, brutalized and had seen many of his friends murdered. He was about to give up when he created a vision. He saw himself, years after the war, standing in a university lecture hall, teaching the lessons of Auschwitz. This vision helped him survive. There was now meaning in his suffering. He had to teach others what had happened and what he had learned. He wrote about this experience in his book, *Man's Search for Meaning*.

What is your overall vision for your life? Is it to excel at sports, study botany, rescue animals, write a play? This vision is larger than the difficulty you are dealing with at the moment. Keeping your vision in your mind will help you build resilience.

and now, thanks to the judge who sentenced me to counseling instead of jail, I've become this person who will do good things in my community and be remembered for good works. My life now can bring value to all the horrible things I went through.

My mother tried to be a better parent than her parents were, and she succeeded. I am going to be a better parent than she was.

Bit by bit, things can get better.

Voice of Experience: Bonnie, 28*

I took on too many responsibilities when I was younger. I was dating a guy who was eighteen when I was fourteen and we were already physically involved. His mother used to call me the devil, a whore, you name it, I got called it. I started to become very self-conscious. I ended up pregnant at sixteen. Don't get me wrong here, I love my daughter. Sixteen is way too young to be a mother. I got kicked out of school, left my parents and I instantly became an adult. I used a lot of drugs before this to deal with childhood trauma. I was in counseling for years before I told them what happened to me.

Life would have been easier if I had talked to someone about what happened and if I would have acted like a teenager when I was supposed to, instead of taking on so much responsibility when I was so young.

Don't bottle up what has happened because it's not your fault, but now it's your responsibility to move past. Don't forget but heal and move past it. If you're sixteen, then act like you're sixteen, not like you're twenty-five. You're only young once.

I didn't deal with my hurts which turned into drug habits, which turned into jail sentences. Now I am in prison. When I wake up in my cell every day all I get to look at is pictures of my children, because I was selfish. I only get one phone call a week to them. I just got

* Written in response to a questionnaire sent by prison chaplains.

transferred from a prison out west to one on the other side of the country, because of my negative associations and decisions. Ten thousand miles away from my family, friends, my life, just so there's a chance that I can change and become the mother I need to be. That's the hardest thing about my life now.

If you're a kid in trouble, confide in someone you trust. There are people who love you and care about you. Don't act older than you are, because shortly you will be that old and you can never go back in age.

REFERENCES AND RESOURCES

Adams, Lee. "Kids." *Bye Bye Birdie* (book by Michael Stewart, music by Charles Strouse). 1960.

Allard, Pierre. *A Little Manual of Restorative Justice*. Public Safety Canada, 2018. www.publicsafety.gc.ca.

American Academy of Pediatrics. "Health Care Issues for Children and Adolescents in Foster Care and Kinship Care," *Council on Foster Care, Adoption, and Kinship Care, Committee on Adolescence and Council on Early Childhood*, Vol. 136, No. 4, October 2015.

Angelou, Maya. *I Know Why the Caged Bird Sings*. Random House, 1969.

A Survival Guide for Teens Aging Out of Foster Care. 2016. www.youthrightsjustice.org.

Bernstein, Nell. *Burning Down the House: The End of Juvenile Prison*. New Press, 2014.

Canadian Council on Learning. A now-defunct organization that studied and collected data about lifelong learning.

CASA for Children. "Domestic Violence Has Long Range Consequences." 8 February 2017. www.casaforchildren.wordpress.com.

Centre for Justice and Reconciliation. An organization that promotes restorative justice around the world. www.restorativejustice.org.

Chiefs Assembly on Education. "A Portrait of First Nations and Education." Assembly of First Nations. 1–3 October 2012. www.afn.ca.

Child AbuseWatch. A resource center for learning about child abuse protection. www.abusewatch.net.

Contenta, Sandro, and Jim Rankin. "Report Shines Light on Poverty's Role on Kids in CAS System." *Toronto Star*, 15 August 2016.

Covenant House. An organization that provides housing and support services to youth facing homelessness. www.covenanthouse.org.

Cunningham, Alison, and Linda Baker. "Little Eyes, Little Ears: How Violence Against a Mother Shapes Children as

They Grow." Centre for Children and Families in the Justice System, 2007.

Dillon, Sam. "Study Finds High Rate of Imprisonment Among Dropouts," *New York Times*, 8 October 2009.

Foundation for a Drug-Free World. An organization that empowers youth and adults with factual information about drugs so they can make informed decisions and live drug-free. www.drugfreeworld.org.

Frankl, Viktor E. *Man's Search for Meaning.* Beacon, 1959.

Gaetz, Stephen, Bill O'Grady, Sean Kidd and Kaitlin Schwan. "Without a Home: The National Youth Homelessness Survey." Canadian Observatory on Homelessness Press, 2016. www.homelesshub.ca.

"Jailing Innocent Kids," *Toronto Star* editorial, 7 September 2016.

Johnson, Harold R. *Firewater: How Alcohol Is Killing My People (and Yours).* University of Regina Press, 2016.

Knowlton, Paul E. *The Original Foster Care Survival Guide.* iUniverse, 2005.

Macdonald, Nancy. "19 and Cut Off," *Globe and Mail*, 28 December 2018.

Marteney, Ken. *Foster Care: A Survival Guide.* CreateSpace, 2012.

Mehta, Vinita. "Growing Up with a Mentally Ill Parent: 6 Core Experiences," *Psychology Today*, 5 September 2017.

Modern Slavery Research Project. A research project that develops research and training to help victims of modern-day slavery. www.modernslaveryresearch.org.

National Clearinghouse on Family Violence, Canadian Women's Health Network. Provides information on all forms of family violence. www.cwhn.ca.

PrisonJustice. An organization that supports prisoners and prison justice activism. www.prisonjustice.ca.

Roosevelt, Eleanor. *You Learn by Living: Eleven Keys for a More Fulfilling Life.* Harper, 1960.

Swift, Richard. *Gangs.* Groundwood, 2011.

Until the Last Child. An organization that supports child welfare agencies to provide for children in care. www.untilthelastchild.com.

What It's Like Going into Foster Care. www.imafoster.com.

Wilde, Oscar. *Children in Prison and Other Cruelties of Prison*

Life. Murdoch, 1897.

Williams, Mimi. "Preventing Jail with Diplomas," *Vue Weekly*, 2 January 2014. www.vueweekly.com.

Zill, Oriana, and Lowell Bergman. "Do the Math: Why the Illegal Drug Business Is Thriving." n.d. www.pbs.org.

ACKNOWLEDGMENTS

It is not easy to share our stories, to admit to the hurts that have been done to us and the hurts we have done to others. It takes courage to look at our lives, learn from our past and dedicate ourselves to a brighter future.

I deeply appreciate the cooperation of the young people, families and voices of experience who shared their stories in this book, as well as the help of experts who have provided contacts, information and vetted the manuscript for accuracy. I would also like to thank Shelley Tanaka and the Groundwood gang for putting this book together.

Deborah Ellis is the author of more than two dozen books, including *The Breadwinner*, which has been published in twenty-five languages. She has donated almost $2 million in royalties to organizations such as Women for Women in Afghanistan, UNICEF and Street Kids International. She lives in Simcoe, Ontario.